Mysticism, Death and Dying

SUNY Series
in
Western Esoteric Traditions

David Appelbaum, Editor

Mysticism, Death and Dying

Christopher Nugent

STATE UNIVERSITY OF NEW YORK PRESS

Production by Ruth Fisher
Marketing by Theresa Abad Swierzowski

Published by
State University of New York Press, Albany

© 1994 State University of New York

For information, address the State University of New York Press,
State University Plaza, Albany, NY 12246

Library of Congress Cataloging-in-Publication Data
Nugent, Christopher.
   Mysticism, death and dying / Christopher Nugent.
      p. cm.—(SUNY series in Western esoteric traditions)
   Includes bibliographical references and index.
   ISBN 0-7914-2205-4 (alk. paper). — ISBN 0-7914-2206-2 (pbk. :
alk. paper)
   1. Mysticism. 2. Death—Religious aspects—Christianity.
I. Title. II. Series.
BV5083.N84 1994
248.2′2—dc20   93-50159
                                                                  CIP

10 9 8 7 6 5 4 3 2 1

This essay is dedicated to the memory of two women, both of whom have illuminated the night. First, to my mother, my first and most enduring teacher. Secondly, to a woman I never met in this life—if indeed she can be called a woman—for she is the gallant teenager who was the first inspiration of this book. As to how, we shall see in Chapter 2.

Oh night, you were my guide!
Oh darkness, lovelier than the dawn!
Oh night, that joined the beloved and her lover,
Transforming the one into the other.

—St. John of the Cross, "The Dark Night"

The discovery of death is that which reveals God to us, and the death of the perfect man, Christ, was the supreme revelation of death, being the death of the man who ought not to have died, yet did die.

—Miguel de Unamuno, *Tragic Sense of Life*

All mysticism, even the darkest mysticism of the Cross, is anticipatory glory.

—Hans Urs Von Balthasar, *The Glory of the Lord.*

To be embalmed with the Divine Nature itself . . .

—John Donne, *Devotions*

CONTENTS

x　　　　　　Contents

FOREWORD

I tell you most solemnly,
when you were young
you put on your own belt
and walked where you liked;
but when you grow old
you will stretch out your hands,
and somebody else will put a belt around you
and take you where you would rather not go.
                                    —John 21:18

We are all dying. And if we are "ultimately concerned," or concerned with "last things," we are all theologians. Accordingly, this little book is intended for all
who are ultimately concerned, not just for those who feel
led where they "would rather not go."

Theology as used here is theology in the original
sense, that is, knowledge as experience of God. If you will,
this can be equivalent to mystical theology, a term especially useful when we are sounding the *mystery* of death.
And mystical theology might above all be commensurable
if we would fathom—which is hardly the same as understand—an underlying and mysterious affinity between
mysticism and death.

This work can be read on two levels. First, it can be
read as an introduction to and speculative essay on mys-

ticism; second, it can be read as a direct application of a mystical spirituality to the inevitable experience of death and dying. I prefer to think of it as an initiation as much as an introduction—that is, as a spiritual experience. The subject is so elemental and universal that, happily, we can avoid technical language. We address ourselves simply to women and men of good will.

The essay would address the whole person, that is, the appeal is to the intellect as well as the will, the head as well as the heart. The concern is "to know" *and* "to be," to know something and to be something. "Practice," as we say nowadays, is always implicit, sometimes explicit, and it presumes that a person is not just concerned with "how to" but with "why." A good physician not only prescribes but explains.

To be sure, the author is not this physician, but only a plodding intern of *the* Physician: The one who said we will know the truth, and the truth will set us free. And if this is so, as Roy, a lifetime disabled friend, put it, "*Truth is a consolation.*" Truth can be a consolation, even the pain of one's own truth, no matter if not first perceived as such. Psychology *alone* is not invariably the consolation it can first appear. Psychology is honored herein, but secondary and implicit. This is first spirituality, and foremost spirituality as grace-in-crisis. Sprituality is, finally, life-in-the-midst-of-death.

The Western literature on death and dying does not go back to the last generation, of course, though important were its contributions. The literature really goes back to the "art of dying" (*Ars Moriendi*) genre of the late Middle Ages. This essay can be seen as a contemporary variant of the older tradition, happily without woodcuts of *le danse macabre*—the dance of death. It would not appeal to fear so much as disarm it, while at the same time reserving for it a health respect. And it is less devotional than it is mystical, while acknowledging that the best of devotional religion, as in a Francis de Sales, is also mystical. In this sense it may not be just contemporary but classic for, in some sense, the original Christian theology is mystical. We would appeal from the "caste" of language to common experience.

The essay is of three integrated and ascending (or descending) parts. Chapter 1, "Initiation: The Mystery of Death," after laying down its foundations, explores an underlying and paradoxical affinity between mysticism and death. It avoids what we might call "cultic thinking," with its too often crude and disastrous *equation* of love and death, on the one hand and, on the other, a more conventional mutual *exclusion* of the two. The latter is more likely, of course, to be the problem. To decondition our deeply ingrained divided consciousness, whether the consequence of popular dread or rationalist reduction, various means of cultivating a unifying vision are introduced. These include "the coincidence of opposites," "the wound of love," and "seriocomic theology," including a "koanistic" sense of Judeo-Christianity.

Chapter 2, "Illumination: Nocturne," presents us with the paradox of enlightenment as a "darkening." Here is brought out the nocturnal side of mysticism and the luminous side of death. This invites revisioning, and if Dante had the poet Virgil to guide him through the darker realms, we shall turn to some of the great spiritual masters, especially "the Mystical Doctor," poet and mystic St. John of the Cross. Suspending appearances, John would show us that God is most present when least apparent, as in "the dark night of the soul." In this context we review prayer and contemplation, and discover companions of passage. We contemplate prayer-as-life in the persons of two extraordinary women, Thérèse of Lisieux and Etty Hillesum. "Illumination," hopefully, should condition us to see, as it were, in the dark. And to see through the dark.

A complete mysticism is not about consciousness ultimately as much it is about life, and life eternal. A Christian mysticism is about a mystical incorporation into the life of Christ extended through and beyond time. This is the part of Chapter 3, which moves beyond enlightenment to love, even to "Immolation: The Sacrifice." Herein is addressed the vacuum of meaning in contemporary life and death, and the ancient rite of sacrifice is introduced as a means of universalizing life and de-alienating death. Love establishes value, and sacrificial love eternalizes it. Among others, Catherine of Genoa incarnates it. Christ, climactically, is both guide and goal. We end, venturing intimations of what "eye has not seen, ear has not heard."

Death and its denial is ecumenical, so will be this essay. Let us conclude our preliminary reflections by savoring one of the great sentences of the century, the final sentence of Ernest Becker, *The Denial of Death*, written with likely cognizance of his own, finalizing cancer:

> The most that any of us can seem to do is to fashion something—an object or ourselves—and drop it into the confusion, make an offering of it, so to speak, to the life force.[1]

Becker has bequeathed us not just an intellectually compelling essay, but an invitation to a sacrifice of self, an all but eucharistic beginning. And as we shall see, he has anticipated our finale, "Immolation: The Sacrifice."

Ecumenicity extends to the employment of scripture and our Biblical citations are from the Authorized King James Version, the Revised Standard Version, and the Jerusalem Bible.

Acknowledgments might begin by allowing that this work is done in collaboration with the wisdom of the ages, and is not, therefore, entirely my own. I owe a special acknowledgment to the indefatigable outside readers of the State University of New York Press, whose scrutiny and suggestions resulted in a substantial improvement of the manuscript. Remaining idiosyncracies, whether of understanding or of style, including incomplete sentences, are entirely my own. The Hospice of the Bluegrass enlarged my knowledge of and sensitivity to the processes of death and dying. And thanks so much to Lynn Hiler for typing the manuscript.

I also want to thank outside readers Daniel Dombrowski and Mary Giles for their advice.

1

Initiation: The Mystery of Death

The mystery of love is greater than the mystery of
death.

—Oscar Wilde, *Salomé*

The more it wounds, the more it heals . . .

—St. John of the Cross, *The Living Flame of Love*

Prefatory

The affecting thought from the finale of Wilde's
strange, sad drama may be wiser than he ever dreamed,
and not just because it echoes the Song of Songs and its
"love is strong as death" (8:6). It is a theological statement, intended or not, and it is the faith of this essay.
Further, it is the faith of this essay that in some sense the
mystery of love and the mystery of death are one and the
same mystery. And this premise has potential to open before us a unifying vision not only stronger than death but
older than death. That is, it can access primordial life before death.

This essay is a mystical interpretation of death and
dying, in the "dark night" of which it would "initiate" us
into the divine vision: To see the way God sees, to think

1

the way God thinks, to love the way God loves. By no means does this presume any special revelation, for we are not without sufficient record of the way God sees, thinks, and loves. True, initiation into "the mind of God" has its potential for self-delusion, perhaps a reason that the exercise of this part of the biblical record, the mystical dimension, has often been reserved to the monastery. "Nocturne," a major symbol of mystical passage in this essay, was in fact at one time part of the first office of the new day, recited at midnight or in the darkest early hours—and it may be time to translate it from the cloister to the world. As Flannery O'Connor wrote in her letters, *The Habit of Being*: "Right now the whole world seems to be going through a dark night of the soul."[1] And, as I think she knew—having been cut down early by lupus—these words have special application to death and dying. But death and dying, in von Balthasar's words, can be "anticipatory glory."

If any of this should seem intimidating, be assured that mysticism can be very ordinary. That is, like death, it is accessible to all. We shall try to see how much like death mysticism can be.

What Is Mysticism?

First, what really is "mysticism"? A mysticism that could be defined would not be very mysterious, and mysticism *is* mysterious. If mysticism, especially as it might relate to the scriptures, is *not* mysterious to the reader, then he or she can forego this foundation and advance immediately to the following section, "Mysticism and Death." I usually begin my seminars on mysticism and spirituality by suggesting that the students check their dictionaries at the door. Mysticism is both exclusive and inclusive, and nothing that can be said about it exhausts it. The classic formulation is "direct experience or knowledge of God." But this tells us nothing of the character of this knowledge, experience, or, of course, of God. Indeed, the idiom of mysticism is paradox, and it is both the beginning and the end of religion. That is, properly understood, religion begins in theophany, the divine apparition or revelation, as, for example, the Burning Bush, and *ends* in theophany, the divine apparition or revelation. In terms of sacred literature, we know the latter as the Book of Revelation. Mysticism returns to the source, anticipates the end, and—should it be necessary to add—respects the "middle," that is, it respects history, itself a mysterious vehicle of more than human disclosure. As Marc Bloch puts it, "Religious experience is historical experience." Time is vital but provisional.

Mysticism has been likened to molten lava that, upon crystallizing, becomes religion. This is by no means intended to slight religion. Both are really complements. Mysticism without religion is apt to put itself beyond judgment, reducing itself to either individualistic or rationalistic "metaphysical" speculation at best: of occult chicanery at worst. Accordingly, some religionists have sometimes held mysticism as suspect, "beginning in mist and ending in schism." But religion without mysticism is subject to its own perils. Religion without mysticism or a depth spirituality can reduce to arid moralism, on the one hand—an overdose of the "thou shalt nots"—or to external habit, on the other. Given this, it is small wonder that many religiously sensitive personalities have foresworn institutional religion. Moreover, mysticism may have its charismatic or pentecostal variants, and it is both ironic and sad when the two, mysticism and the charismatic/pentecostal, see only the *aberrations* of the other, identifying the first with "navel-gazing" and the second with hysteria, when *in principle* they are expressions of a common Spirit. It is not the Spirit which is divisive! This anomaly is rather Matthew Arnold's "ignorant armies" fighting "by night," or what I have elsewhere characterized as "the demon of division." Like any spirituality, mysticism is a gift of the Holy Spirit, but its accent is upon the relatively less dramatic gifts, like wisdom. The mystical accordingly is likely to be more open to wisdom traditions universally than the charismatic and, ironically, expressed more by silence than by tongues. But the two meet, or should meet, in nurture of the greatest of the gifts: Love. If the word *mysticism* is still objectionable, one may simply call it spiritual or contemplative theology.

But the reality, as over against the word, is another thing and, I submit, a biblical thing. This is only another way of saying, as I hope we shall see, that a Christian mysticism, while perhaps introducing unfamiliar language (because, as indicated, it is language all too often reserved to the monastery), in principle complements rather than contradicts a more basic "evangelical" conversion. *Ideally*, the mystical can in fact presuppose the evangelical—and possibly vice versa. This construction may be the sense of an obscure passage in Hebrews (6: 1–3) about leaving "the elementary doctrines of Christ" and going "on to maturity." It is small wonder that the challenging figure of the mountain pervades spiritual literature.

The main point of the foregoing is to affirm the inherent compatibility of the mystical and the evangelical. This compatibility is in principle demonstrable in the person of St. Francis of Assisi. Francis, "the herald of the great king," may be the greatest "evangelical" of the medieval world; and interestingly, as the recipient of the stigmata has also been considered the person who had the greatest mystical experience of that very mystical age. And if we can believe Bengt Hoffman, *Luther and the Mystics* (1976),[2] there is something mystical about the founder of the Evangelical Church. More generally, the mystical side of the Reformation is seen in its radical fringe, e.g., the Quakers. Regardless, soon enough the two spiritualities, the mystical and the evangelical, were estranged by mutual incomprehension. My own sense is that the best people now wear the conventional labels rather lightly, preferring ecumenical common nouns to sectarian proper nouns. Scripture is intended presumably to open, not close, ourselves.

We shall draw upon the treasures of the Western mystical and spiritual traditions, allowing them to fix our meaning of the terms. And this is a tradition, I submit, as rich as any, though it has suffered much from the anti-contemplative bias of our pathetically preoccupied and rationalistic modern world. Our foremost classic is, of course, the Bible, and both the Old and New Testaments are replete with mystical experience. One of the first great mystical experiences is, as suggested, that of Moses and the Burning Bush (Exodus 3:1–15), but we might, for simplicity's sake, see our mystical tradition descending historically from Abraham's departure by faith for a promised land (Genesis 12:1). Abraham put Western religion firmly "on the path," as is said nowadays, but for the mystic the promised land is not so much territory without as it is a temple of the Spirit within. And if we might appropriate St. Augustine, we get there "not by steps, but by love."

Still, mysticism is not just a pietistic "religion of the heart," but one of the whole person. And a Christian mysticism is not just concerned with Christ-worship but with Christlikeness. Years ago the English Benedictine, Dom Aelred Graham, asked his terrible question, "Have we substituted Christ worship for being Christlike?" Recourse to the debris of our history leaves little room for doubt. It seems evident enough and perhaps human enough that we have elevated Christ on a pedestal, distancing Him from ourselves, conscious or not, *as a rationalization for not following Him.* This observation is not by any means to tamper with Christ's divinity, only to suggest something of the vagaries of *our* humanity. We are only human. Yes, and the human Christ may be a bit too intrusive.

Nothing of this dynamic is to suggest that mysticism is an "athletic" spirituality that sets itself above the lesser breed. It requires, as we shall see, not so much effort as assent. It demands not so much dogged attachment to some heroic agenda as it does detachment. This is simply a "letting be," as Meister Eckhart had it, to what we really are.

But what are we? This is another mystery. The human is a creature who shoots the moon but does not really know himself; indeed, fears himself—and rightly so—if an awesome Kingdom *is* within. In fact, our shadowy and repressed *fear* of self-knowledge has been seen by Abraham Maslow[3] as Sigmund Freud's greatest discovery. We may mask fear of our destiny with a diversionary panic of activity, becoming that estranged creature who defines itself by what one does rather than by what one is—not much comfort when one is unable to do very much. Fortunately, we are more than we do, and even more than we seem. We may not always look like it, but we are made in "the image and likeness of God," affirmed even after the Fall (Gen. 9:6); and the aim is to *realize* this image and likeness. This kind of self-realization may entail, paradoxically, self-effacement. Paul is a great evangelical theologian, but he is also a mystical theologian, and he illuminates the matter of self-effacement in one of the most magnificent passages of scripture:

> And we, with our unveiled faces reflecting like mirrors the brightness of the Lord, all grow brighter and brighter as we are turned into the image that we reflect (2 Cor. 3:18).

If Paul is intimating that ours can be a destiny that is more than merely human, John, one of the most mystical of sacred writers, is more explicit:

> My dear people, we are already the children of God, but what we are to be in the future has not yet been revealed; all we know is that when it is revealed, we shall be like him (1 John 3:2).

John is, of course, the evangelist of "indwelling" and "abiding." And he not only writes of the unity of Christ and the Father, he maintains that *we* should have the same kind of unity with Christ as does Christ with the Father. And that this is not just verbal or even moral unity is suggested by Paul's very "prayer," one of the most astonishing passages of Holy Writ—and astonishing not just in its content but, regrettably, in its neglect:

Out of his infinite glory, may he give you the power through his Spirit for your hidden self to grow strong, so that Christ may live in your hearts through faith, and then, planted in love and built on love, you will with all the saints have strength to grasp the breadth and the length, the height and the depth; until, knowing the love of Christ, which is beyond all knowledge, you are filled with the utter fullness of God (Eph. 3:16–19).

Paul here is balanced, yet bold, and in a single sentence, he has given us a synopsis of mystical theology.

Let me in passing call our attention to just five points. First, Paul is describing a process not an instant solution, a process that is clearly a gift, a grace: "may he give you." Obviously, this denotes no claim to what C. S. Lewis called "inherent luminosity." Secondly, "your hidden self" alludes to a distinction between appearance and reality, a distinction that goes back at least to Paul himself (Rom. 7:16–22). It is widely known in our time, especially through the influential writings of Thomas Merton, as the distinction between the true and the false self, with the latter being a mere psychic illusion or social construct. It is a mask, yet we *are* more than we seem. And we are more than we seem for more than one reason, because, thirdly, we are a part of a larger body: "all the saints." God's gift has a communal character, a prudent counterweight to any pretensions of our all too naturally imperious egos. Fourthly, we are called to "knowing the love of Christ," something "beyond all knowledge." This disavowal of intellectualism reinforces the communal character of the previous point, affirming that the experience is at least as accessible to the simple as it is to the savant. It is also an oblique but clear expression in Paul himself of what is generally known as negative theology, which is the substance of our next chapter and which we can defer until then. Fifthly, and climactically, Paul concludes with his awesome phrase, "filled with the utter fullness of God," something for which he obviously felt no need to apologize. But this, generally known to theology by such technical terms as the Eastern Church's *theosis* (literally, "filled with God") or "divinization," is consummated *in glory*—i.e., on "the other side"—another counterweight to the mundane chicanery and manipulative reveries of potential supermen. Generally, Paul seems to avoid language as bold as "the utter fullness of God," but when he says that the "mystery"—and please note that word—is Christ "in you" or "with you," (Col. 1:27) he is maintaining *essentially* the same thing. He is declaring that the "incarnation" is not just unique and singular, pure and simple, but a continuing, historical process. Put inclusively, he is speaking not just of incarnation, but of "incorporation." This incorporation is but an application of the Pauline doctrine of the "mystical body of Christ," lent perhaps a new pertinence. The standard formulation descending from the Church Fathers corroborates. As Athanasius phrased it, "The Logos was made man so that we might be made God."[4] But divinization is a process of grace, not of nature, for grace *is* illimitable. Let us again note that our mysterious vocation is fulfilled in glory.

Paul bespeaks an extraordinary experience, but a mystical experience is not necessarily Pauline. That is to say, it is not necessarily like the dramatic experience Paul had en route to Damascus. We might well find this fortunate; after all, Paul was blinded. An authentic mystical experience is not necessarily—and this is an understatement—the experience that *we* might be looking for, for example, an experience of unalloyed bliss. We are all too suggestible. And we may have a real mystical experience and not understand it till much later, which is another way of saying that we may have such an experience and not necessarily know it at the time. This is not because it is so ordinary—though the mystical genius is in reality that of the ordinary and unaffected, and not the "esoteric"—but because *we* are ordinarily so spiritually insensitive and myopic. The spiritual is just the deepest part of ordinary life. It is "deep" calling to "deep" (Ps. 42:7), that is, it is the "deep" of God calling the depths of humankind. In such matters, spiritual direction is very helpful. Ignatius Loyola, himself a spiritual master, seems to have spent a lifetime divining, or digesting, if you will, the meaning of his great experience at Manresa. Mystical experience, then, is not a substitute for mystery or for faith, but is itself mysterious. It is dialectical or inclusive, and it deepens mystery even while it illuminates it. It enlarges horizons, including our awareness of their infinity.

We have illuminated, it is to be hoped, in some foundational way, what is intended by the term. To recapitulate and enlarge, mysticism, while inexhaustible, is or is like:

A practical art, more concerned with being than knowing. Still a "science," or as Evelyn Underhill once characterized it in her standard, *Mysticism*, "the science of reality." It distinguishes appearance from reality, including the appearance and reality of the self, retrieved by self-effacement. Having broken with surface value, having never been estranged from the source, being the Source, it is the arbiter of appearance and reality.

"Dialectical" or inclusive "logic," venturing beyond *apparent* contradiction to deeper and mysterious unity. Paradox, and paradox that forswears mere reason for something deeper and richer.

Liberation *and* conformity. Liberation from self. Conformity to love.

In the beginning, "heart trouble." Shipwreck.

Union by love. Being *in* Love. Being-in-Love.

"He must increase, but I must decrease" (John 3:30).

A spirituality not just of sainthood, but of Christhood.

The Zen koan, or riddle to break through vain intellectualism and induce enlightenment, wherein the disciple asks, "Who is the Buddha?" and the master replies, "Who are you?"

"Seeing the way God sees . . . " Therefore, Zooey in the climax of J. D. Salinger's gem, *Franny and Zooey*, breaks through to his overwrought sister, Franny, by the revelation that we ought to shine our shoes for that most homely, unsung, and *apparently* least mysterious of creatures, the anonymous "fat lady"— for "the fat lady is Christ."[5] This is not vulgarization but vision. And if the "virtuous" object that they did not see Christ, the Gentle One's irrefutable reply is insofar as you did this to the least" of these, "you did it to me" (Matt. 25:40).

It begins, then, with vision, which may be no more than taking another look. Shall we?

Mysticism and Death

The author would be the first to acknowledge that, theologically, there is nothing especially novel in the fore-going section. But when we build upon its foundations and advance to the subject of mysticism and death, we may be venturing into a relatively unexplored horizon. That there is an intimate connection between the mystery of death and mysticism is an essential conviction of this essay. At first sight this claim might appear implausible, and for several reasons. First, by the end of the seventeenth cen-tury, mysticism was generally reserved to "extraordinary" experience—a grace of the privileged few—and there is nothing more apparently *ordinary* than death. Whether a consequence of this kind of theological constriction or not, something of a theoretical vacuum was created, and sen-sational popularizers rush in where religious profession-als fear to tread. Popularizers too readily confound mysticism and the occult.

Modern culture, increasingly dominated by popular culture, has suffered from a vulgarization of mysticism.

Mysticism has come to mean whatever one wants, which means it is no longer very mysterious. In some circles it is reducible to, if you will, *Dancing in the Light*, I dread to say, even if its author, Shirley MacLaine, has brought pleasure into the lives of many people. But everywhere in the contemporary spiritual marketplace there is a one-sided and insidious *fixation* upon the pleasure principle: upon light (a light that is all but palpable), euphoria, psychological and physical well-being, the rationality that forecloses a healing initiation into the deeper ironies of Carl Jung's "shadow," and above all St. John of the Cross's "dark night of the soul." Euphoria, for one thing, readily obscures moral sense. Naturally, everyone wants light and euphoria, but a fixation upon them anesthetizes rather than conscientizes. The thing is to seek God, not euphoria. And God, of course, is not necessarily euphoric.

Popular spiritual fare lacks what Rudolph Otto, in a famous book, *The Idea of the Holy* , characterized as the *mysterium tremendum* and the *mysterium fascinans* , a confrontation with the overwhelming mystery that fills us at once with dread *and* fascination. A synthesis of the two might subsist in "awe." Awe, even more than joy, may be the ultimate religious emotion—and awe is inclusive of joy. Moreover, there is in the spiritual marketplace a confusion of what the spiritual masters call "secondary effects" with mysticism proper. Secondary effects are such things as real or imagined visual experiences, trance states, and out-of-body experiences. One can have these without mysticism, and mysticism without these. They can be artificially induced by drugs and by other means, but the great masters would say that a mystical experience cannot be induced. We can and ought to be disposed to it, but we cannot induce it. The infinite is not mechanically at the disposal of the finite.

Given the foregoing prejudices and predispositions of popular culture, the idea of a connection between mysticism and death might understandably seem strange. Death is not a very marketable commodity. Still, our connection has been glimpsed or understood by various mystical writers, though I have never seen it articulated in any systematic way.[6]

We speak of "the mystery of death." The very word *mysticism* seems rooted in death. That is, it has remote associations with "the mysteries," the pre-Christian esoteric and exotic cults whose objective was immortality and which flourished in the ancient world. Since official religion was more of an arid state cult, civic in its ends, it could not meet the deeper needs of the people, especially with the inevitable ebbing of political morale in the later Greco-Roman world. Accordingly, "the mysteries" represent, among other things, a popular outlet for emotionality and an effort to come to terms with the riddle of death. They had, for example, primitive rituals of rebirth. But they also had, ironically, rituals of castration.

Enter to these mysteries the apostle Paul.[7] Paul was fully aware of the vagaries of the mysteries, including some of their magical and lurid practices, but he legitimated *the term*, only infusing it with a new content and meaning. Paul, as it were, offered a corrective to the vulgarized spiritual fare of his day, obsessed as it was with "signs and wonders." To the spiritually starved, anxiety-ridden pagan world, he proclaimed that *the* "mystery (*mysteriōn*) hidden for ages" had at last been fully revealed, and revealed as the experience of Christ (Col. 1:26). "Mystery" was rendered from the Greek into the Latin *sacramentum* and the English "sacrament," itself rooted in the Greek verb "to initiate." Accordingly, in our sacrament of initiation, baptism, Paul can proclaim that, to underscore our connection, we are "baptized into his death" (Rom. 6:3). To which he adds, encapsulating the longing of humankind universally—a longing sung by Dante as that for *La Vita Nuova*—that we might have "a new life." Thus is this mysterious "new life" rendered inseparable from death. Death can be seen, on the one side, as *the* centrality of religion, as the centrality of the Paschal *Mystery* of the Easter liturgy attests.

Rationalism may find something objectionable in this kind of accent, viewing it as confirmation of its own worst suspicions that religion is a human invention and a desperate, if not puerile attempt, to evade the menace of death. I do not know how many rationalists there can be in the face of something as "unreasonable" as death, but the concern here is not to evade death but to confront it. But, as we have suggested, religion *begins* with the mystery of death, and the modern classic of the irrepressible Miguel de Unamuno, *Tragic Sense of Life*, makes an unforgettable case study that, in this respect, nothing has changed in the intervening millennia. Still, rationalists are right and perhaps even more inspired than they know to expose the neurotic potential of religion, what the prophet of the death of God and self-styled "antichrist," Friedrich Nietzsche, called the petty and craven *ressentiment* of so many of his complacent religious contemporaries. And religion, like anything else, is in perpetual need of purification and reform.

Religion is about more than death. And death, to be sure, is to be resisted as well as accepted. The record for the resistance to death of the growing martyrologies of, say, Latin America, make this painfully manifest. Among them one can hardly avoid mention of Oscar Romero of San Salvador, slain at the altar in 1980. His very last words were from the text that could well serve as our leading motif: "Unless a grain of wheat falls into the earth and dies, it remains alone, but if it dies, it bears much fruit" (John 12:24). The point is that death is a religious experience and, potentially, a mystical experience.

The allusion to mystical experience can serve to get us back on track with the mystery of death and mysticism. Let us contemplate the "logic" of mystical union. And let us risk simplification, for reality is more subtle than logic. There are various types of "union with God," including a strictly "natural" union, enjoyed by all humankind, for existence is theologically unthinkable without God holding us in being. But if "mystical union," as it were, a real presence to the Real Presence, a consciousness of communion, "a timeless moment," is more than a natural union—and I submit that this is the consensus of the spiritual masters—where or when is *full* union with God and the Blessed to be realized? *In death*. If this is the case, mystical experience is or can be a foreshadowing of death. Or as von Balthasar put it, mystical experience is "anticipatory glory." A foretaste of heaven is what we allude to, and it would seem that there cannot be a foretaste of heaven without a foretaste of death. And the constitution of humankind is such that it cannot endure full union and survive. We are as bubbles—and the bubble would burst. This is only to say that mysticism and death are very close. As St. Thérèse of Lisieux, whose life was dramatized in a beautiful film some years ago, described her mystical experience: "I burned with love and felt that one more minute, one more second, and I would be unable to bear the fire without dying."[8] There are even pagan variants from classical mythology. Semele *was* burned to death because she unwisely insisted upon seeing Jupiter.

This construction of a subterranean connection between mysticism and death seems consistent with both scriptural and historical texts. The Jewish scriptures, of course, understandably, against the background of the pagan milieu and its confusion of God and humankind, stressed the transcendence of God: God the Creator as "the Other" standing over and above the creation, the divine inviolability, the divine remoteness. Scripture is not a scientific tract, fortunately, but an art and profuse with all the ambiguities of art. Therefore, Isaiah, in his great mystical vision, can proclaim, "I saw the Lord Yahweh seated on a high throne" (6:1), but the more constant refrain is that "no one may see God and live." And Isaiah, by the way, seems almost to have himself perished in his experience: "I am lost" (6:5). Moses, in the theophany of the Burning Bush, covered his face, "afraid to look at God" (Exod. 3:6). When Moses is later emboldened to ask to see God's glory, he is informed: "Man cannot see me and live" (34:18–20). This is the characteristic refrain of the Old Testament (Exod. 19:21, Lev. 16:2, Num. 4:20), applied even to hearing "the voice of the living God speaking from the heart of the fire" (Deut. 5:26). The holy was so sacrosanct that if even an animal touched the sacred mountain it was to be stoned (Exod. 19:13). Still, transcendence, I hope it goes without saying, is not to imply a polarized "dualistic" or childlike "vertical" conception of heaven and earth: "Heaven and earth are filled with your glory" (Isa. 6:3, as enshrined in the *Sanctus*). Heaven begins here.

With the incarnation and the New Testament, there is a rather novel accent upon the immanence of God, God-with-us; moreover, Jesus of Nazareth is the most accessible of men. But the glorified Christ of the Resurrection is more mysterious in his comings and goings, appearing and disappearing unaccountably, as all but a ghost, allusive of the older affinity of mysticism and the mystery of death. He had had his own "initiation" into death. Paul's extraordinary experience on the road to Damascus did not result in more than death of the "old man," but it was enough to blind him for three days (Acts 9:9). And when in Corinthians he alluded to a mystical experience fourteen years earlier he could still not determine whether it was "in the body or out of the body" (2 Cor. 12:2). At the very climax of the New Testament, the old association is confirmed: "When I saw him, I fell at my feet as though dead" (Rev. 1:17).

Martyrdom reinforces the affinities between mysticism and death. Traditionally considered the most privileged Christian death, Karl Rahner denominates martyrdom a suprasacrament—sacrament being, in the Augustinian formulation, "a visible sign of invisible grace." This certainly holds for the first Christian martyr, Stephen, and for some of the early fathers. Rarely has the mystery of death and mysticism been so intimately and even visibly related as with Stephen. At the very act of being stoned, he cried out: "Behold, I see the heavens opened, and the Son of Man standing at the right hand of God" (Acts 7:56). His mystical vision and his moment of death were synchronic. The evolution of mysticism has been seen in direct continuity with the history of martyrdom. That is, when the "red" or material martyrdom of the saints abated, with the age of Constantine and toleration, the vacuum was filled—direct experience of God—by the "white" or metaphorical martyrdom of *mortification*, by a dying unto self. This takes us beyond logical to linguistic affinities, and they are profuse, as the term *mortification* can suggest. Most relevantly, the Latin for both "ecstasy" (*excessus*) and "rapture" (*raptus*) are derivative of forms of the verb, "to die."

We have progressed from the scriptural record to the historical record. Or if you prefer, we have progressed to the continuity of revelation in time. And here I believe we shall find a continuing evidence of our connection, at least in the classic texts of some of the greatest mystical experiences. I shall cite but three.

The first is the great experience of St. Augustine (d. 430) and his mother, Monica, at Ostia. The text, incidentally, seems one of relatively few of a joint mystical experience. Augustine begins in his *Confessions* by indicating the setting: "Now the day was approaching on which she was to leave this life . . . she and I were standing alone, leaning in a window which looked onto the garden." But after having made the setting so concrete, he continues:

> Our talk had reached this point: that the greatest possible delight of our bodily senses, radiant as they might be with the brightest of corporeal light, could not be compared with the joys of eternal life. . . . Then, with our affections burning still more strongly . . . we raised ourselves higher and higher and step by step passed over all material things . . . and we came to our own souls, and we went beyond our soul to reach that region of neverfailing plenty. . . . So we said: if to any man the tumult of the flesh were to grow silent, silent the images of earth and water and air . . . if there were silence from everything . . . and . . . He Himself alone were to speak . . . would not this be: "Enter into the Master's joy"? (IX,10)[9]

The experience is indeed mysterious, and Augustine can deal with it only by indirection. But our point is that Monica shortly *did* "Enter into the Master's joy" (incidentally, alluding again to the great text of Matt. 25:31–46).

That is, after the experience her joy was complete, and she several times asked, "So what am I doing here?" It was her *Nunc dimittis*—"Now dost Thou dismiss Thy servant" (Luke 2:29). And within approximately a week she had departed. It is as though the mystical experience and her own experience of mortality were two parts of one process.

Our second experience is that of St. Francis (d. 1226) at Mount Verna, and it has recently been deemed by Ewart Cousins as the greatest mystical experience of the Middle Ages,[10] a very mystical age. This is his famous stigmatization, the reception of the wounds of Christ, themselves witnessed by contemporaries. Interestingly, this also occurred towards the end of his life, and after his reading an account of the Passion. His earliest biographer and contemporary, Thomas of Celano, recounts that Francis saw:

> in *the vision of God* a man standing above him, like a seraph with six wings . . . fixed to a cross . . . the sharpness of his suffering filled Francis with fear . . . and so he arose, if I may so speak, sorrowful and joyful . . . and while he was thus unable to come to any understanding of it and the strangeness of the vision perplexed his heart, the marks of the nails began to appear in his hands and his feet, just as he had seen them a little before in the crucified man above him.[11]

There is so much that could be said about this experience. Francis, as it were, painted with the stigmata, has become almost an icon of Christ. The figure in the vision parallels our earlier one of Isaiah (6:1–7). We might add that the larger text indicates that the experience was preceded by the prayer of Francis not just to worship Christ, but to be *like* Christ, even to the point of the Cross. The wounds of the stigmata represent a mystical sharing unto Christ's death. And the experience of Francis at Mount Verna can be seen as his synthesis of that of Mount Calvary and the mount of the Transfiguration

(Matt. 17: 1–8), possibly the greatest mystical experience of the New Testament.

One aspect of the experience of Francis has general import and calls for an elucidatory aside. The text seems to speak all but unconsciously of a peculiar coinherence of "fear" and joy: Francis "arose, if I may so speak, sorrowful and joyful." The text's author need hardly apologize for an *apparently* ingenuous and naïve expression of a sophisticated theological truth.

This truth is "the coincidence of opposites." This great truth, like mysticism, can be "ordinary" experience, i.e., accessible to all. William Blake saw it essentially as second nature for children and saints. Great emotion, as for example, at a wedding, is likely to be a coincidence of opposites ("sorrowful and joyful"). A rainbow is a product of a coincidence of opposites, i.e., of rain *and* shine. Poetry, as opposed to prose, is likely to inscribe a coincidence of opposites. A great mystical experience is assuredly a coincidence of opposites.

The "logic" of the coincidence of opposites is inclusive and existential rather than categorical and notional, and it is a mystical logic. That is, it is a decidely mysterious logic, such as "the first will be last" and of Christ *as* "the first and the last" (Rev. 1:17). The logic of the coincidence of opposites respects *both* ontological unity ("coincidence") *and* empirical plurality ("opposites" even). Opposites can magnetize, and the coincidence of opposites accommodates both focus and infinity, harmonization and "horizons." Like anything else, including Holy Writ, this kind of logic is subject to abuse. The doggerel of the violent denizens of Anthony Burgess, *A Clockwork Orange*, for example, *confounds* life and death. There is a proper androgeny *and* gender confusion. Mircea Eliade, in his seminal *The Two and the One*, goes so far as to speak of the "satanic hermaphroditism"[12] of Aleister Crowley, a jaded magus lionized in occult circles in the 1960s. In light of the perils of normlessness and anarchy, mystical logic must be understood in context—inclusive of its "works."

Our great formulator of the coincidence of opposites was, of course, Nicholas of Cusa (d. 1464). As bishop, mystic *and* scientist he was also something of its enfleshment. God, Cusa perceived, was a coincidence of opposites, e.g., transcendence and immanence; again, in the Christian dispensation, "one" and "three, i.e., singular and plural."[13] Our late incarnation of the coincidence of opposites was Thomas Merton (d. 1968). Merton was more poet than theologian (or a theologian in the original sense), but he could on occasion conceptualize a mystical experience as follows:

> This realization at the apex is a coincidence of all opposites (as Nicholas of Cusa might say), a fusion of freedom and unfreedom, being and unbeing, life and death, self and non-self, man and God. The "spark" is not so much a stable entity which one finds but an event, an explosion which happens as all opposites clash within oneself.[14]

Language is predicated of boundaries, and Merton is adumbrating a bracketing or collapsing of boundaries: Totality. And as Anthony Padavano wrote of Merton and, I believe, of mystics universally: "Nothing is clear because everything is present."[15] In short, clarity is sacrificed to comprehension. And clarity is sacrificed to depth. Mystical enlightenment is not just about clarifying obscurity but obscuring premature clarity.

Let us now return to our texts, so we might better appreciate how, in Francis's experience, the saint was "unable to come to any understanding of it." Even seers "see through a glass darkly." But *we* might now be better able to understand that admixture of fear *and* joy, which is really awe, perhaps the highest religious emotion. And it is awe, fascinatingly, that characterizes so many faces in the religious art of the later Middle Ages.[16] *After* the great age of the mystics, the more saccharine (*or* lacrimose) conventions predominate. The preservation of creative tension that is second nature to mystical logic has dissipated.

One should also note Merton's coupling of "life *and* death" (emphasis added). Interpenetration of life and death pervades the text of Francis, who died, incidentally, two years after the experience. We have, of course, espied this factor in St. Monica in the text from the *Confessions*. This coinherence of life and death would seem, finally, to undergird generally our advancing an association of mysticism and death. But strictly speaking, the two associate as a coincidence of opposites. To impetuously dissolve the tension between the two is to court death, not mysticism. Death "dissolves," as does, unfortunately, a divorce a marriage; it is *mysticism* that is a coincidence of opposites. We best regard both unity and distinction. The irreducible mystery subsists in how mysticism and death could not be closer together—or farther apart.

In studying mysticism we do well to focus not so much on concepts as on their incarnation in mystics. And fortunately, we are amply endowed to illustrate these early ruminations.

For example, our third and final text is from the Spanish golden age mystic, St. Teresa of Avila (d. 1582). And Teresa is a peerless exemplar and prolific mother of mystics. Like so many women of genius, even if a happily ordinary genius, she was a relatively late bloomer and went through a long "desert experience" of some fourteen years in which she could scarcely meditate at all. But she became one of the most experiential of mystics and greatest masters of prayer. The following text is that of her "transverberation," translated into marble by the famous sculpture of Bernini:

> It pleased the Lord that I should see . . . an angel in bodily form. . . . He was very beautiful, his face so aflame that he seemed to be one of the highest types of angel who seem to be all afire. . . . In his hands I saw a long spear and at the end of the iron tip I seemed to see a point of fire. With this he seemed to pierce my heart several times so that it penetrated my entrails. . . . He left me completely afire with a great love of God. The pain was so sharp

that it made me utter several moans; and so excessive was the sweetness caused me by this intense
pain that one can never wish to lose it, nor will one's
soul be content with anything less than God.[17]

If mysticism can begin as "heart trouble," as we have
intimated, the transverberation of St. Teresa is a "heart
attack."

Of course, the candor and the curious detail of her account, including the "intense pain" and the "sweetness,"
have incited suspicion in some quarters, leading to
Freudianized postmortems about the "sexually repressed"
Teresa. But students of Teresa come to know her as among
the least repressed of women. And as we shall eventually
underscore, the *language* of mysticism is, and for good
reason, the language of love. The late and eminent R. C.
Zaehner put it well:

> There is no point at all in blinking the fact that the
> raptures of the theistic mystics are closely akin to
> the transports of sexual union, the soul playing the
> part of the female and God appearing as the male.
> But the human relationship is the symbol of the di
> vine, not, as the psychologists hold, the divine of the
> human.[18]

In other words, human love simulates divine, not the reverse. But of course, our direct concern here is not the
symbolism of Eros, but that of Thanatos, the death symbolism in the piercing of Teresa's heart. And she, most interestingly, according to observers, was granted the
supreme gift of dying from and in a state of mystical rapture.[19] With her, the mystery of death and mystical
experience becomes not analogous but virtually indistinguishable. One might also note, once again, her own embodiment of the coincidence of opposites in the
coinherence of pain and peace.

It would be tempting at this point to advert to the
contemporary world and its growing literature on what
we know as near-death experiences (NDE), as a kind of

linchpin for our thesis. But this I am presently reluctant
to do. Certainly some of the saints, including Teresa, had
experiences that would qualify as near-death experiences,[20] but when I look at contemporary accounts, I do
not see experiences of the same quality as those of the
saints. Of course, this may be more than we should expect
from near-death experiences, but I do not yet detect the
same sense of awe in our accounts of near-death experiences. Moreover, they seem to be structured in a mechanical rather than in a "moral" (or free) manner. This
may owe something to the transcription of the experience,
not the experience itself. Certainly, when in a coma or under anesthetic, the unconscious yearnings of the deep self
can be very receptive. And, admittedly, some of the differences may be explicable as reflecting the difference of
our culture from that in Spain during the age of Teresa. I
think that we should continue to welcome studies in this
area, but it would seem that we simply do not yet know
enough about these experiences, and I shall accordingly
pass up the opportunity to apply them here. In any event,
we do not really need them here, for the more traditional
evidence seems already ample to our thesis.

There is at least one more evidence of an association
of the mystery of death and mysticism, and this is one of
the *apparently* strangest of all. We allude to the desire for
death, found widely with the mystics and, admittedly
again, in many of the near-death experiences, at least immediately upon "return" from the experience. This is, if
you will, a kind of mystical, not neurotic, death wish. It is
likely to be as transient as the mystical experience itself,
but its memory lingers, inspiring trust. The experience of
the desire for death seems to be premised upon the experience that, after the mystical heights, all mundanity can
taste of ashes. We might also venture that, if one has
"seen the glory," all can be enhanced, another application
of the coincidence of opposites. The common point is that
the desire for death expresses not *necrophilia*, but
theophilia; not the love of death, but the love of God. In
Christian theology the thought goes back at least as far

as Paul's, "I want to dissolve and be with Christ," *adding*, "but for me to stay alive in this body is a more urgent need for your sake" (Phil. 1:23–24). Perhaps this is a variant of the Buddhist idea of the bodhisattva, who, though spiritually realized, forgoes nirvana in order to put himself at the saving disposition of "all sentient beings." Or perhaps the bodhisattva is a variant of Paul? In all events, the desire for death is marked in countless mystics, including Dame Julian of Norwich, St. Teresa, St. John of the Cross, and the ingenuous John Bunyan of *Grace Abounding*. "The Mystical Doctor," John of the Cross, has expressed this in a marvelous verse from which I, at least for the moment, shall content myself with quoting only the stanza:

> I live without living within myself,
> And in such a way that I
> Keep dying because I do not die.[21]

Whether essential by now or not after this, let us conclude these observations with this affirmation: The point of these reflections on the mystery of death and mysticism is not so much that a mystical experience can be like death. It is rather that death can be like a mystical experience.

A Note on the Problem of Evil

With all this mystery, some may wonder why we are not addressing what philosophers of all ages have often considered the greatest mystery of all: The mystery of evil, "the problem of evil." If God is good, why should there be evil? If God is great, even omnipotent, why should there be the apparent evil of suffering, especially innocent suffering? This is, to be sure, no place to review the answers to that great conundrum (koan) that have come down to us from the Book of Job through St. Augustine to Charles Hartshorne. But then the solution to a koan is not an idea but an experience. For example, an experience of someone who also suffered unjustly—someone who came not to solve the problem of our suffering with a syllogism, but to enter it and live it with us.

Compassion has its reasons that reason knows nothing of. And the mystery of love, with its promise and its power of reweaving all in glory, is the voiceless and maybe ultimate response to the mystery of evil.

The Wound of Love

"The mystery of love is greater than the mystery of death." The former has thus far been more implicit than explicit, but it is suffused and secreted throughout the essay and made most manifest in Chapter 3. Language, or its superfluity, can have its way of cheapening the deeper realities, which values are perhaps best preserved with a certain reserve. Moreover, it may seem unlikely that there is anything new to be offered on a subject as old as love. Here again the reality is prejudiced by the appearances, as in the seductions of popular culture, for example, with "soaps," as a consequence of which love may not always look like love. The reality, as Dostoyevsky put it so inimitably in *The Brothers Karamozov* is that "love in action, as against love in dreams, is a harsh and dreadful thing." All mothers experience this, as may most of the rest of us, if late.

This the great mystics have always understood. Their abiding motif is "the wound of love," and their classical text is the Song of Songs, one of the shorter books of the Bible but the one that has compelled, perhaps, the most mystical commentaries. Rarely in literature is found such a mixture of erotic, innocent, and mystical love. But the bride of the Song of Songs is "sick with love" (2:5), and she has suffered its famous "wound" (5:7). Love is or can be a "wounding" because ultimately the willingness to undergo suffering for one's beloved is the measure of one's love.

Love is not only a wounding, but a kind of "death." It represents the loss of self in another—or for another. This has glorious antecedents in the song of the suffering servant of Isaiah, "by whose wounds we are healed" (53:5), bequeathing us the paradox of the wounded healer. And, in his fine study, *The Kiss Sacred and Profane*, Nicolas Parella suggested that "The One who was first wounded by love was Christ on the cross."[22] But it is St. Augustine, that most exuberant and quotable dynamo of theology, who brings the wound of love and the experience of "mystical marriage" together:

> Like a bridegroom, Christ came forth from his chamber, and with a presage of his nuptials he went into the field of the world. He bounded like a giant exalting on his way; he reached the marriage-couch of the Cross, mounted it, and there he consummated his marriage.[23]

This *is* a love even stronger than death (Song of Songs 8:6), a healing love that may, incidentally, have its unmined affinities with homeopathy.[24]

In popular myth, the wound of love survives as a *motif*, innocuously enough, in the shafts of Cupid of our St. Valentine's day. But it was enshrined gloriously in the stigmata of St. Francis and the transverberation of St. Teresa. Few of us may welcome it, but we might be wise to ready ourselves for its intrusion.

And the moral of these reflections is not that love is like death, but that death is or can be like love.

Reflections to the Reader

Let us be more personal: Death is not strictly academic. The great Jewish theologian, Abraham Heschel, once spoke of death as "a privilege." None of us may be worthy of this privilege, but we must either accept if we can or reject if we must the "gift" of the present moment that is offered us. Mystics remind us that "the present moment" is the only one we have. Living in the moment is in fact the biblical way of living: "Let the day's own trouble be sufficient for the day" (Matt. 6:34). It may also be a privilege to know that we are confronting our own climax. This makes death come less as a "thief," more as an awakening, even if a rude one. It allows us to become what we should have always been, and in some sense really are. It would allow us to discover, or rediscover, the wonders of the ordinary: Cat's-paws, Spanish shawls, the sunset in the bay. Active anticipation can compel us to simplify our lives, which can be to spiritualize our lives. And it can make the present moment precious—the "acceptable time." As Paul would put it: "Behold, now is the acceptable time; behold, now is the day of salvation" (2 Cor. 6:2). Now *is* an acceptable time to disarm an inexorable and involuntary "second death" (Rev. 2:11) by ourselves freely electing in this life upon an even more fundamental and moral *first* death, the death of the ego. We can, as it were, cast a rehearsal.

Rehearsal can be a fit metaphor. I myself have felt that what is probably a lesser known film of Ingmar Bergman, *After the Rehearsal*, is really his artistic testament. To me it is to cinema what Hermann Broch's masterpiece, *The Death of Virgil*,[25] is to literature. It is heavy with world-weariness, and in it the artist sounds, if not the vanity, then the insufficiency of art. Its climactic line is, I think, "Everything represents, nothing is." And we are eventually called to gaze not into the nihilistic void, but away from it to that-which-is, to the "I AM." This is to be like Moses. It too is privilege.

No one knows what death is like, but I think it can be something like love, even sexual love, when we let go of ourselves, and naked, vulnerable, but trustingly, pass over into the other. To pursue the figure, "Sister Death," as St. Francis called it, can be like a pregnancy, an unwanted pregnancy. But an unwanted pregnancy can still be a "gift," a mysterious gift. Pregnancy is one of our greatest spiritual metaphors: "When a woman is in labor she has sorrow, because her hour has come; but when she is delivered of the child, she no longer remembers the anguish, for joy that a child is born into the world" (John

16:22). This text has been seen as embodying the whole of the spiritual life.

We write not just for "the expectant mother." We are all dying, and seen "from above," that is, from the Eternal, "a thousand years in thy sight are but a yesterday when it is past" (Ps. 90:4). "Ask not for whom the bell tolls," sang John Donne, "it tolls for thee." An ancient antiphon of the ninth century put it incomparably: *Media vita in morte sumus*; that is, "in the middle of life we are in death." Thomas Aquinas is said to have wept at these words. And it is no accident that Dante begins *The Divine Comedy*: "In the middle of the journey of our life . . . " "Our life," not his life. But his original title was simply *La Commedia* ("the comedy"), for it begins in sorrow but ends in joy—in fact, in a mystical experience. Luther reversed it well: "In the midst of death we are in life." This is only the coincidence of opposites in its temporal form: Spirituality's great paradox of "simultaneity." We *are* contemporary with Christ. We are contemporary with him who said: "Before Abraham was, I AM. He *is* with us "always."

Reflections on the Ecumenicity of Death

Fear of death is natural. Or maybe it is supernatural. That is, it has been intimated that there is relatively more fear of death in the conventionally more "supernatural" Judeo-Christian West than in the more "natural" or "mythic" religious cultures of antiquity, the Native American, or the Orient. The distinguished Protestant theologian Oscar Cullmann, for example, himself went so far as to contrast the serenity of the death of Socrates with that of Jesus himself.[26] In some Eastern religious cultures, suicide, not just euthanasia, has at times been spiritual counsel.[27] And the ever-popular Ram Dass (Richard Alpert), in one of his tapes, can dismiss death as "taking off the tight shoe." However well intended, I am not sure that this does adequate justice to the mystery of death. On the other hand, if we can enlist Dylan Thomas, hardly a representative figure of Christian orthodoxy, there is his: "Rage, rage against the dying of the light."

If there are essential differences concerning death between the great religious cultures, there are also differences within them, and we should be guarded about generalization. All the same, let us attempt a few speculations. We might first suggest that, in distinction to the doctrine of "apathy" (*apatheia*) inculcated by the more radical Stoics, Christianity, as the daughter of Judaism, not only accepted passion but even celebrated the centrality of the Passion. It was fully licit to feel what one feels. Just as the Incarnation affirmed the reality of the world, Christianity early rejected Docetism, the notion that there was anything illusory about the humanity of Jesus. He was not, as poet Edwin Muir put it in his reply to Nietzsche, some actor at Golgotha, "miming pain,"[28] the illusion of death and dying. Whether perceived as Platonic or otherwise, *maya*, the world-as-illusory, is generally alien to Western religion.

Foundational for the Passion of Christ, itself a centrality of Christian art, of course, was the Judeo-Christian postulate of the *person* and the person as a body-spirit unity. This assumption is itself basic to the value of the individual, a word anchored, interestingly, in "indivisible." Such a rich notion of the individual as a unity ought, in principle, to invite some reconsideration of more than just popular ideas about "dualism." A counterweight to the value of the individual, if you like, is what I think of as our carrying "the burden of the body." Not just a physical burden for us all, the body was a philosophical burden for Paul in Athens. That is, when he went beyond the Greek idea of the immortality of the soul to the Christian idea of resurrection in his historic proclamation there, the body proved something of a stumbling block to the Greeks (Acts 17:32). The reaction of the apparent majority of the Athenians can imply a certain abhorrence of the body and an unavowed dualism, peculiar in that place of the body beautiful. No doubt those "Epicurean and Stoic philosophers" (Acts 17:38) would rejoin rather that Paul was proclaiming a philosophy of the absurd. Paul, preacher of folly (1 Cor. 1:18–25), would probably congratulate them upon the observation, only maintaining that a philosophy of the absurd alone can take the full measure of death—and sometimes of life.

Let us simply suggest that the body is not the least of our mysteries. It is part of what even some physicists now ponder as "the bottomless interiority of matter." Source of pride and shame, pleasure and pain, even horror, the body is destined not just to the charnel house but to glory. But we see the glorified or "spiritual body" (1 Cor. 15:44) through a glass darkly. We know not what kind of "body" this is. Maybe differences between immortality and resurrection are marginal, and maybe not. If theologies make a difference, our being irrevocably wedded to the body would seem to provide underpinnings for our attitudes toward the passion of death and dying.

Let us now attempt to enlarge upon and apply some of this. Two considerations can stand out, and they seem to reduce to respective apprehensions of, in some sense, space and time. Space concerns humankind and the cosmos: time concerns humankind and, of course, *chronos*. The West, especially the rootless modern West with its tenuous sence of place, is deemed relatively more oriented around time. Antiquity, the Native American, and some Eastern cultures are deemed relatively more oriented around space. Space is spacious, if you will, and seems so naturally all-absorbing or dissolving that distinctions about humanist and personalist values can pale into insignificance. The product of this mindset can be a "softer" sense of self, with relatively less of self to *lose* at one's inevitable demise. Frederick Holck observes that, especially in Hinayana Buddhism, the "I am" has "no ontological status." The realization of this "renders one immune to the fear of death since there is really nothing which death can attack."[29] As Stephen Levine puts it in one of his well-received titles, *Who Dies?*[30]

Our second and correlative consideration concerns time. The West is generally held to be more historically minded—more fixated on time than on nature. This originates with Western religion. With Judeo-Christianity, time was linear and limited. In fact, we sometimes even speak of St. Augustine, our first great philosopher (or theologian) of history, as "inventing" time, i.e., defining and specifying "time" as simply that finite period between the Creation and the Parousia, the endtime. Time was invested with finality, and it was above all denominated by the Fall. Death was, as it were, a microcosm of a larger finality. In this perspective, death was not just natural, but a dire consequence of some mysterious and primordial supernatural drama. Death violated our birthright, and it ought not to be. Death represented an "unnatural" interception of a divine order, and it was "the last thing to be destroyed."

Thus have we a foundation for an inimical view of death. And therefore, if Christ, in all his humanity, feared death, as Oscar Cullmann affirms, he may have had reason. And his fear could be a comfort to the rest of humanity.

If some other religious cultures had a "softer" view of the self, they could also have a "softer" view of time. In such cultures nature could subsume time, which could tick off into oblivion. An inkling of this attitude is available in that most atypical and all but oriental book of the Bible, the book of Ecclesiastes. Here the Preacher cries: "There is no new thing under the sun;" "There is no remembrance of former things. . . . The sun also rises. . . . All the rivers run into the sea; yet the sea is not full . . . thither they return again" (1:5–8). If there is more sense of space than of time in the text, if you will, more horizontality than verticality, as has been written, "When there is no time there can be no end of time."[31] To much of classical antiquity and the oriental world, time was naturally cyclical and virtually interminable. And reincarnation was, it seems, among other things the human part of these larger natural cycles. Reincarnation could, of course, mitigate the "sting" of death. And there is an extensive literature, e.g., *The Tibetan Book of the Dead*,[32] for guiding the subject in his or her passage from life to death and from death to life. Sogyal Rinpoche has just published his more contemporary *The Tibetan Book of Living and Dying*,[33] which has received enthusiastic endorsement in the West.

Religious cultures are best served in the long run by learning from each other, but a reminder here and a caveat there might not be unfraternal. If reincarnation is one palliative against the fear of death, Sogyal Rinpoche would support that there is still a respectable fear of death in Tibet. Far more importantly, we do not want to forget that reincarnation was just what the Buddha himself hoped to *void*. He wanted to break, not perpetuate, the cycle of death. Rebirth meant "redeath." In this construction, Buddha would himself be on the side of the party of finality. Some of our Western exponents of reincarnation can trivialize or effect a denial of death. For example, against the setting of inevitable reincarnation, I am reminded of a popular American guru who quipped that "Suicide is impossible." This would not seem appropriate in a culture where the tragedy of suicide is increasingly commonplace. Any trivialization of death inevitably means a trivialization and devaluation of life. To be sure, Westerners have found ample ways to betray life values. Although there is no point here in some partisan declaration of honors, there is something to be said for the biblical view about the finality of time. It renders time precious. Time is invested not just with finality but endowed with teleology, i.e., with purpose and meaning. And therefore passion, as opposed to apathy, is rendered meaningful. Our pledge of this remains *the* Passion.

Nature itself, of course, is mother, but Naturalism is a Pandora's box. Naturalism is the reduction of reality to nature, just as Scientism is the reduction of method to science. Naturalism is neo-primitive. A naturalistic neo-paganism is fashionable in probably mostly ingenuous circles in recent years, but *indiscriminate* reproaches against ultimately, Judeo-Christian humanism ("speciesism"), have potential not just to elevate the animal kingdom but to lower humankind. This is hardly to deny continuum in creation or to countenance the spoliation of the planet. But to anyone who has lived with it, nature is not just "moonlight and roses" but also "red in tooth and claw." Racists and robber barons understood the predatory and pitiless side of nature, as did indeed the Nazis. "Nature is cruel," observed Hitler, "therefore we too can be cruel."[34] We shall sing of nature and its starry night another time.

As I believe wise men of both East and West will acknowledge, there is such a thing as a wise and prudent fear of death. In his masterpiece, *The Brothers Karamozov*, Dostoevsky had a sinister character portending a virtual counter-apocalypse, a coming-of-age of humankind in which people would forever renounce God. Having become liberated of transcendence, so much would we love each other that this life would be sufficient, and we would no longer fear death (XI, 9). But this character is his own Nietzscheanized *devil*, selling his seductive half-truths.

Nietzsche was, of course, an alienated intellectual whose philosophy of the "superman" (*Übermensch*) put him beyond common humanity. Not so the celebrated Leo Tolstoy, Nietzsche's contemporary. Tolstoy himself wrote compellingly on death in his little novel, *The Death of Ivan Illich*, concerning the final dread of a man who had failed to live authentically. For Tolstoy, as against Nietzsche, authentic life was that *of* common humanity, specifically the peasantry. In his autobiographical *Confession*, Tolstoy confessed unforgettably—despite fame and fortune—his own terror of death and fear of living inauthentically. Reconciliation, including reconciliation with faith, came through his observations on the simple, but genuine, annals of the peasants. Rooted in the soil, free of superfluity and pretense, and supported by the timeless rhythms of religion, the peasantry did not fear death.

Tolstoy, we might add, incidentally relates a charming story of several Russian monks or hermits and their skete, or monastery, in remote Archangel, near the Arctic Circle. They were so unlearned, so simple, that they did not even know the Lord's Prayer. Once the bishop ventured a boat trip in order to pay them a visit, and in compassion for their ignorance, spent an entire day laboriously teaching them the Lord's Prayer. Satisfied at last, he bade them farewell and set back out to sea. But in the dark of night he saw a great, strange light rising on the water. It was the monks, walking on the water, appealing to him with the equivalent of, "Your reverence, what comes after 'Thy will be done?'" And that, by the way, is a question that this essay ponders.

We began these reflections by observing that death is not strictly academic. Let us conclude them by suggesting that, if life is sectarian, at least death is ecumenical. So too would this essay be.

Though framed in Christian terms, the essay is adaptable, should one be disposed to personal appropriation. For example, the Jewish reader might first have recourse to Rabbi Kushner's fine book, *When Bad Things Happen to Good People*. Moreover, one might simply substitute for Christ herein, "the Holy One," or an equivalent. Stephen Mitchell, in his highly acclaimed translation of the book of Job, can render Job's God "The UNNAMABLE."[35] And some might take comfort in that we are now being told that the mystic who more than any other informs this book, St. John of the Cross, was himself a genius of Jewish stock (on his father's side) and a Carmelite, an order which claims descent from the community of Elijah on Mount Carmel. John was thoroughly in love with the Jewish scripture, and his last request was that a brother read to him the Song of Songs, after which he expired. And this was at midnight, or if you prefer, at nocturne. Of course, St. John of the Cross was Catholic, but catholic too, and his spirituality encompasses everything from his declaration about being "born again," at the one end, to, as we shall see, his doctrine of *nada* ("nothing"), with its affinities with the Buddhist doctrine of *anatta*, at the other. Among the most universal of mystics, John's essential affinities extend virtually from Buddhist to Baptist.[36] If one is Buddhist of a more devotional bent, one can keep on practicing one's *nembutsu* ("Buddha-reflection"). Or if one is a Buddhist in its nontheistic form or an agnostic, which can be counterweights to our sometimes too facile talk of God, one can have recourse to Paul Tillich's "God beyond God." In sum, the mystery of God transcends all "God talk." Small wonder that even Karl Barth could describe the task of the theologian as like painting a bird in flight. And I must share his confession that the angels will laugh when they read our theology.

The Comedy of Resurrection

We have risked irreverence here and there, not lest we be accused of undue gravity but perhaps as a memento that our subject is ultimately comic. It is of both *Gravity and Grace*, a suggestive title by Simone Weil—and grace is light. Grace is light, not just light as a feather but, ironically, light as the "fat lady" of J. D. Salinger's *Franny and Zooey*, of whom we have spoken. This fat lady was in some sense "Christ." Grace is fraught with surprises. And not the least surprise is how, while pale reason excuses itself before death, comedy embraces it.

Our subject is as comic as the *Commedia* of Dante for it is, in fact, the same subject. "In the midst of the journey of our life," says the poet of the divine, "I found myself lost in a dark forest." "Our life," he says, striking the universal note, and we can be so lost that we do not notice how beautiful the forest can be. And that maybe we are not lost. The experience of Dante calls to mind a stanza of St. John of the Cross:

> Then if from now on
> You no longer find me among the flock of men,
> Say that I was lost

Love-struck along the way,
But lost only to be found again.[37]

The text is kindred to being not just "lost" with Dante, but comic in the same sense: *We* begin in sorrow, and end, or would end, in joy. It goes without saying that the comic is not synonymous with "funny," or incompatible with seriousness. The seriocomic is still another concidence of opposites—and of life rendered more abundant.

So let us make more explicit the comic mode, and end, at least this chapter, in joy (or maybe a smile). What could be more comic, after all, than the great human comedy of man confusing himself with God—except possibly the Eucharist: bread and/or the body of Christ? And if we do not believe in the Eucharist, as poet James Carroll ironically wrote: "The *bread* believes." And maybe the hungry too, for whom bread can be "divine."

We may protest that the last thing needed right now is some kind of gallow's humor; besides, we still cannot believe in God. Then maybe we could let God believe in *us*. But if we cannot believe in God, we can all, really, believe in laughter. Where there is humor, there is hope, and where there is hope, there is, implicitly, faith. It has never been demonstrated that tragedy is closer to the wellsprings of religion than comedy. This premise, as so much else, seems to go back to Paul, implicit in the Pauline "fools for Christ." If it is implicit in Paul, it is explicit in Erasmus of Rotterdam, who seems to ground his fools not in contrast with "vain philosophy" but in human experience itself. The consequence is "comic theology," with humor a therapeutic and even theological response to angst, or dread. Sir Thomas More can quip while being led up the scaffold, "Help me up if you would, but as for coming down, I will shift for myself." The dying St. Francis, according to legend, requested the brethren to "Bring in the fiddler." So much in character for Francis is this that one can wonder if it were legend. Then there is the dying Zen master who, weary of all the wailing of his disciples, chided them to pipe down so he could hear the gossip of the washerwoman outside the window. One can wonder if it is not the Zen koan as such or its irreducible comedy that can shake one into enlightenment.

One might object that this is too eclectic, and that there are no Christian koans. But *if* Christianity has no koans, it is because it *is* a koan. It is replete with riddles not to be explicated but experienced. Let us enlist some leading examples: The "scandal" of a special incarnation? "Son of God" or "Son of Man"? The first or the last, *alpha* or *omega*? A suffering "God"? The Cross as the "crux," as Chesterton said? What greater koan could there be than the Paschal Mystery—Life through death? Possibly "Before Abraham was, I am" (John 8:59)? What about the mystery of the Trinity? Can you meditate on that for twenty years without a grin (as well as perhaps a grimace)? Going from the sublime to the really ridiculous, is it not a koan that *we* are "children of God"? That sense can be made out of *this* life? That *these* bent and broken "drybones" can be resurrected, or that they should be? That *the mystery of love is greater than the mystery of death*, especially the mystery of divine love? That "God so loved the world . . . " (John 3:16)? *This* World? Can God really say, if no doubt in a weak moment, that "I will have no memory of their sins" (Jer. 31:34)? An absent-minded God? What kind of God is that?

A God of resurrection is that kind of God, of course, and resurrection is the ultimate comedy. Humor is an idiom of "resurrection," and I suspect that this applies to *the* Resurrection and his koanistic "I am the Resurrection." And therefore I am not sure that it is entirely accidental that one can sense glimpses of humor in the post-Resurrection appearances. This has been seen for what is perhaps the most solemn of all the appearances, that of the pilgrims of Emmaus. When, as a gentle older Jesuit father has suggested, Cleopas excitedly says to the Lord: "You must be the only person staying in Jerusalem who does not know the things that have been happening there these last few days," Christ replies, slyly I think, "What things?" (Luke 24:18). Or after the indignity of the Cross, Christ had to endure the ludi-crous indignity of the dumb-founded, doubting Thomas poking around his wounds (John 21:24–28)! Or Mary Magdalene confusing the Risen Lord with a gardener (John 20:15)! Or consider the impetuous Peter at Lake Tiberius, "who had practically nothing on," but "wrapped his cloak around him" *before* jumping into the water to swim to Christ (John 21:7)!

With all this confusion, it is small wonder, as the scripture scholars know, that the Resurrection accounts do not square in all details. And there may be humor in that a Jewish scholar wrote, some years ago, affirming the bodily Resurrection of Christ, at a time when many Christian theologians are denying it, if indeed a few are not embarrassed by it. Not impossibly, a resolution is that the Resurrection appearances of Christ may be mystical experiences. This was the Christ of glory, and we are not accustomed to encountering a glorified body. As we have suggested, high mystical experience is likely to be both obscure and certain. Certainty is not clarity. Finally, if the Resurrection appearances can be understood mysti-cally—which is by no means the equivalent of discar-nately—then there would seem no reason in principle for them to be terminated. As declared even the father of modern scientific history, Leopold von Ranke, "All ages are equidistant from God."

To be sure, "I have been," with Job, "holding forth on matters I cannot understand" (42:3). I have been trying to say that some things are too deep for tragedy and that death may be one of them. If this is the case for the indi-vidual person, how much more might it apply to that of a people, as in the Holocaust? That experience as beyond tragedy, I think, helps account for the bittersweet, serio-comic element in Nobel laureate and Auschwitz survivor Elie Wiesel, as in *A Beggar in Jerusalem*. His sense of the incommensurate is anticipated, no doubt, in some of the koanlike sayings of the Hasidim. For me, however, a very special saint of the Holocaust was the "shining personal-ity" of Etty Hillesum (1914–43), whose miracle was such that she could not hate even the Nazis. Her last recorded words en route to Auschwitz were, "We left the camp singing." This too is resurrection.

Time grows short, and we have probably not yet had our resurrection, much less our mystical experience. There are those who would say that such things are impossible; indeed, that this is a book of the impossible. I am shameless enough to all but consign Nietzsche to the flames and yet quote him approvingly: "Nothing is worth doing unless it is impossible." Especially if it is not something *we* do. I have advanced elsewhere that Nietzsche himself may have been surprised by the impossible, for, after erratic antecedents, on 3 January, 1889, upon chancing to witness a cabman mercilessly beating his horse, Nietzsche, apostle of the pitiless Will to Power, interposed with his own body, and broke down. Or did he break through?

We have ventured beyond exposition to experience and, whether we have succeeded or not, that is what Initiation aspires to do. The great medieval mystic, Meister Eckhart, was once asked, "What is eternal life?" He responded, "Why not ask eternal life?"

2

Illumination: Nocturne

I was afraid to go to sleep, I thought maybe I would never wake up.

—Burlena Turner, *The Lexington Leader*,

8 November, 1982

He grants them some delightful awakening.

—St. John of the Cross, *The Living Flame of Love*

Prefatory

Burlena Turner, in whose memory this book is co-dedicated, was an ordinary fifteen–year–old teenager save for one thing: She had cancer. Suddenly she had cancer. Almost as suddenly, she also found herself abandoned by most of her friends, including a boyfriend, who could not deal with it. She became suicidal. At that point, hospice professionals were called in, and gradually Burlena was transformed. Indeed, this gallant young lady herself became something of an inspiration and transforming leaven in the larger community of Lexington, Kentucky, itself. She died in the blossoming of the following spring and was buried, appropriately, I think, within the week of Easter. Her last words were an act of faith in and experience of God.

But Burlena was, or had been, afraid of the night; therefore, she would stay up most the night watching television. I came to learn that this was not unique to her. Shortly after her passing a next-door (or to be precise, across-the-creek) neighbor died of cancer, no teenager but a gentleman in his later sixties, and he too would sit up through the night and sleep by day. About the same time another gentleman of approximately the same age in the village was similarly afflicted and kept vigil on the porch all night, retiring indoors at dawn. This struck me as peculiar, and there is reason to think that it is based on more than just a fear of being alone; for example, one is even *more* alone on the porch than in the house. To fall asleep, after all, is an act of faith. A hospice professional, Karin, once told me that everyone dies facing the light. If this should prove an exaggeration, it remains one that bespeaks a common experience of humankind.

Universally humankind has feared the terrors of the night. This was above all the case in the old pagan world, and it is problematic how much Judeo-Christianity has done to mitigate it. We are acculturated from the folk tales of childhood and the monster movies of popular culture to think of the "nocturnal" as the realm peculiar to ghosts, phantoms, and demons, the sphere of the irrational, the grotesque, and the lupine. Thus the ancient monks could sing *lauds*, at daybreak, in a hymn of the fourth century attributed to St. Ambrose, the *Aurora jam spargit polum*:

> Away, ye midnight phantoms all!
> Away, despondence and despair!
> Whatever guilt the night has brought,
> Now let it vanish into air.

All this may be reinforced by a conception, or misconception, of the Godhead itself. If "God is light" (1 John 1:5), what then are the likely corresponding affinities of *darkness*? The demonic, we are conditioned to reply. But *is* God "light" or, as in the tradition of St. John of the Cross, an *excess* of light, and therefore, a blinding darkness *to us*? If so—if the radiant glory of the Lord exceeds our capacity—it is above all in the "night" that *we* are to find God. This is the point from which we proceed, hoping to illuminate the character of our "night." And hoping that we might add to the ancient night prayers of the monks the even older promise of the psalmist: "You will not fear the terror of the night . . . nor the pestilence that stalks in the darkness" (91:5–6).

Night and Negative Theology

But first, what is "night"? Enjoying, as it were, a safe conduct of the psalmist, let us risk being drawn into its darkness. What we may find is that it is darker than even we thought, and therefore fertile with more unseen possibility. "Night" is not so much a physical as it is a spiritual or moral category, just as the divine "light" is not so much a physical as a spiritual and moral reality. The divine light is immaterial. God dwells in "inaccessible light." Inaccessible, at least, to the most brilliant devices and machinations of our will.

Night, then, is more than the negation of day but, interestingly, a powerful metaphor for "negative theology" (or variously, "the way of negation," the *via negativa* or apophatic theology). This is an ancient and honorable tradition whose lineage goes back to personalities like the Alexandrian Jew and contemporary of Christ, Philo; it was articulated for Christianity by a great church father of the fourth century, Gregory of Nyssa; and it was enshrined in one of the shortest but most influential spiritual documents ever written, the *Mystical Theology* of Dionysius the Areopagite, once considered a direct disciple of Paul but believed to be a Syrian monk of the fifth or sixth century. From here it came down to Meister Eckhart, a misunderstood spiritual genius of the German high Middle Ages, shaped *The Cloud of Unknowing*, a famous but anonymous work of late medieval England; and

finally, some would say, climactically, was taken over by
the great mystical doctor of the Spanish golden age, St.
John of the Cross. This is not just a Western but a universal tradition, with its variants in Sufism (Islam), Buddhism, and Hinduism. Its universality and its appeal to
common human experience should enhance its credibility.

Negative theology is premised upon the transcendence of God. That is, God is postulated as "beyond": Incomparable, invisible, ineffable, indescribable. The old
pagan deities could be too anthropomorphic, and Ignatius
of Antioch declared that if God were like us, we were lost.
The God of negative theology is an image of God not to be
depicted in graven images. It is God beyond all linguistic
and logical categories, not to be grasped by reason or
sense, but by the *negating* of reason and sense. Ironically,
it speaks of illumination by darkening, of "knowing by unknowing." Enlightenment, it will be recalled, is not an
idea, but an experience. It is less information than trans-
formation. Negative theology speaks not so much of what
God is as what God is not, and after it has eliminated
everything that God is not, it comes at last to what God
is. It comes at last to the pure "I AM."

If this procedure should sound novel, the premise of
negative theology was part and parcel of the faith of the
fathers. It would bracket the objective in religion in order
to enhance experience of the mysteries of faith. The theological substance of the negative way is enshrined in what
George Tavard calls the "remarkable formula" of the
Fourth Lateran Council of 1215: "Between the Creator
and the creature one cannot find a resemblance without
finding a greater dissemblance."[1] This is no theological
conceit, of course, but an essential counterweight to what
seems the human propensity to reduce God to an object.
The subtle reserve of the negative way was effectively sacrificed to the more "populist" impulses that dominate
modern piety. Modern devotionalism, no matter how endearing, is likely to be moralistic and antimystical. Modern piety is generally "positive theology." It is likely to
reduce the mysteries of the faith to credal propositions

and piety to more or less prescribed prayer styles and to provide a ubiquity of conventional religious images that, paradoxically, leave little to the imagination. One needs only enter a baroque church to experience the latter. Or, need one add, listen to some Evangelical sermons for the linguistic equivalent.

Against the context of the modern, then, negative theology can be revolutionary. It not only stands for the recovery of the mystical ("knowing by unknowing") but can also fly in the face of more sophisticated and elaborate scholastic theologies. But, as we shall suggest, the two theological traditions are best seen as complementary. The ironical premise of the negative way is affirmation by denial, and it is cognate with the coincidence of opposites. For example, with negative theology "Less is more." It functions by subtraction, not by addition. Michelangelo, once asked how he made a block of marble look like a horse, replied that he cut away all the stone that did not look like a horse. It is a spirituality in which *silence* speaks louder than words. It is spiritual "minimalism."

All this is abstract. Let us try therefore to render it concrete with the help of a story. The best illustration I have ever had the pleasure to encounter is from the charming collection of stories known as *The Little Flowers of St. Francis*, contemporary stories weaving fact and legend about Francis and his first disciples. The story concerns Brother Giles, a favorite of Francis, and St. Louis, King of France, both of whom were something of legends in their own time. The story relates of how St. Louis was journeying through Italy, determined to have a meeting with Giles, whom he had never met. It goes on to tell how Brother Giles was called from his cell and ran to the gate, whereupon:

> without asking any questions, though neither had ever seen the other, both of them hastened to embrace each other, kneeling together very devoutly and exchanging an affectionate kiss, as though they had been intimate friends for a long time. Despite all

this, they did not say anything to each other, but re-
mained in that embrace, with those gestures of loving friendship, in silence. And after they had stayed
that way for a long time without saying a word, they
separated. And St. Louis continued on his journey,
and Brother Giles went back to his cell.

Giles, questioned by the friars why he had passed up the
opportunity to speak to such a great king, responded:

Dear Brothers, do not be surprised that neither he
nor I was able to say anything to each other. . . . By
God's grace we looked into each other's hearts, and
whatever he thought of saying to me or I to him, we
heard without sound made by lips and tongue even
better than if we had spoken with our lips—and with
great consolation. . . . Because of the defect of human
language, which cannot clearly express the secret
mysteries of God except by mystic symbols, that con-
versation would have saddened rather than consoled
us. And so you should know for sure that the King departed marvelously consoled.[2]

The point of the story, of course, is not the little miracle alluded to, but "the defect of human language." Language was simply not equal to the occasion. It was not, as
it were, good enough. No doubt we have all, on special occasion, experienced something of the more or less in-
stinctive turn of these saints to silence. Their silent
embrace, resonating with meaning, is a telling metaphor
for negative theology.

The peculiar dynamic of negative theology can be
further illuminated by contemplating the difference between knowledge and wisdom—the latter seeing the way
God sees, thinking the way God thinks. Knowledge can
be deemed a product of "inclusion;" wisdom, of "exclusion." That is, knowledge is acquired by "ingesting" a
body of intelligible material; wisdom, on the other hand,
is more likely a consequence of "fasting," elimination,
concentration. And, of course, of suffering. I am not sure

if this has ever been put better than by Aeschylus, great dramatist of ancient Greece, in one of the holiest lines of all literature:

> Even in our sleep, pain, which cannot forget, falls drop by drop upon the heart, until, in our despair, against our will, comes wisdom, through the awful grace of God.

If knowledge is acquired, wisdom is infused or is given, and theology calls it a gift of the Holy Spirit. The fruit of negative theology, wisdom, is knowing by unknowing, by something deeper than knowing. Wisdom is knowing by a more elemental "sympathy," literally a "suffering with," in lieu of an externalizing of, opposition. This kind of wisdom at least is inseparable from love. Rarely have I seen it more movingly expressed than by J. F. Powers, *Wheat That Springeth Green*: "there was something to be said for whatever it was, charity, or despair, or a blend of both— wisdom?—that moved old men to silence."[3] The coin of a Christian wisdom is apt to be the self-emptying *folly* of the cross (1 Cor. 1: 18–25), our most common if unavowed symbol of the coincidence of opposites.

"What you have come to is nothing known to the senses," says the author of Hebrews (12:18). To this we might append: Nothing known to the intellect. But lest we be rendered senseless, prey to the irrational and the unreal, let us issue a cautionary before proceeding. Negative theology involves a kind of "blackout," not because it "prefers darkness to light" (John 3:19)—which it assuredly does not—but because the naked eye cannot grasp or endure "light inaccessible." Negative theology can be among the most universal of spiritualities because it avoids all the particularities of history and of culture. It is theocentric, or centered upon God, or to use the counterpart from philosophy, centered upon the Absolute. Generic theism does not necessarily presume that all "gods are created equal." There are "savage gods," as our century has certainly illustrated, and an *inverted* and *false* mysticism (not to go into some of the more fratricidal and inquisitorial episodes of conventional religion) has from time to time been enlisted into their service. This is notoriously the case with Nazism.[4] Of course, the perils are not usually anywhere so drastic, but in the very first sentence of *The Cloud of Unknowing* its anonymous author seems to qualify its charm by issuing a dire warning against even mentioning the book to anyone deemed unable to use it with good will and profit.[5] The likely perils can emanate from a kind of vertigo where one's idea of reality is called into question, of turning inward only to find oneself and confounding it with more than oneself. So there are perils to "taking the path," but there are also perils to *not* taking the path. Thus there is always the more sinuous alternative of spiritual atrophy.

For these reasons, negative theology is best exercised within the context of a more "positive theology" (the way of affirmation, *via positiva*, cataphatic theology). We need not be intimidated by language: Positive theology is essentially the objectifiable in religion, and it is likely to be whatever religious matrix in which we were raised. After all, God *is* revealed as well as hidden, manifest as well as mystery. The positive way is more oriented to a distinctive personal God, particular rites, sacraments. Unobstructed, the two, positive and negative, really flow into each other and are dialectical complements. Positive theology can provide an institutional, communal, and scholastic safety net (and much more, too) to the nocturnal side of religion, but if it shuts off negative theology, it can preclude authenticity, stunt spiritual growth, and make of the heart a stone. Negative and positive theologies are, of course, coincidences of opposites.

The significance of the foregoing can be reinforced by anticipating the later section on meditation, for positive and negative theologies have their respective prayer styles. The point is that one's inherited devotional tradition is reducible to mere external habit, and that prolonged aridity, or even irritability, in ecclesiastically prescribed prayer or the equivalent need not mean that

one is losing one's faith; it may mean, rather, that the time
has come to augment one's prayer style and to deepen
one's faith. It may represent a summons not so much to
"put away the things of a child," as it were, but to adopt
the things of an adult. It can be symptomatic of a time not
to abandon prayer but to deepen it. Spiritual aridity can
be ironically "deep" calling to "deep" (Ps. 42:7). It summons us not so much to move on but to move up. It can bid
us to take a "higher seat" at the wedding banquet, as
Christ might say. That, at least, will be our assessment.

Our procedure is simple enough. First, to repeat, our
consideration of negative theology involves the counterweight of a positive theology, the latter of which will be
the dominate mode in the next chapter. Second, having
experienced some *initiation,* we shall in this chapter attempt an *illumination* of nocturnal theology, until, in the
last chapter, we contemplate a unifying *immolation.* This
procedure is only to bend to our purposes the traditional
"purgative," "illuminative," and "unitive" stages. To be
sure, these stages are descriptive more than prescriptive,
and they can be simultaneous as well as sequential. Moreover, there is no final state of rest to the soul in this life.
Third, and finally, we shall sit as students of the masters,
and let us hope that we are now ready to experience one
of the greatest, St. John of the Cross.

Remembering one of the least, with whom we have
been so bold as to pair him, Burlena Turner. We have not
lost sight of her "night." We are entering it more deeply
and fully, to see what we might find there.

St. John of the Cross

St. John of the Cross has a system, but it is an open
system of "inward form." By "night," a key metaphor, he
means at least three things: First, faith, which is "night"
to the light of natural reason; second, affliction, whether
spiritual or sensual, as one is the subject of purification

or catharsis; and third, God, a darkness to our natural faculties.

Night is a metaphor for mystical theology, that is, Christian theology in the original sense of the term. In distinction to a discursive and linear scholastic theology, mystical theology here is "an inflowing of God into the soul." Mystical theology is *mysterious* theology, and it is "received" rather than "acquired," that is, it is gift, a grace. Let us reproduce a remarkable passage from *The Dark Night of the Soul* (V, v, 1–3), wherein John opens by announcing that:

> This dark night is an inflowing of God into the soul, which purges it from its ignorance and imperfections . . . and which is called by contemplatives infused contemplation or mystical theology. Herein God secretly teaches the soul and instructs it in the perfection of love, without its doing anything, or understanding of what manner is this infused contemplation.

But why, John asks, is "the Divine light" called a "*dark* night"? Essentially, it is because of "the height of the Divine Wisdom, which transcends the talent of the soul, and is in this way a darkness to it." He goes on, explaining:

> The clearer and more manifest are Divine things in themselves, the darker and more hidden they are to the soul naturally; just as, the clearer is the light, the more it blinds and darkens the pupil of the owl, and, the more directly we look at the sun, the greater is the darkness which it causes in our visual faculty.[6]

This is an idea as old as Plato's *Republic* and as contemporary as walking out of a matinée at the cinema into the blinding sun. It is light, but until focused and habituated, it is darkness *to us*. John's light is the same as Paul's, as when he spoke of his great conversion experience at Damascus: "The light had been so dazzling that I was blind" (Acts 22:11). Still, this may be the kind of light that, as we say, "the blind see." By faith John really means *faith*, indispensable to loss of ego. We might best think of it less as an indiscriminate "blind faith" than as unconditional trust. It is less intellectual than it is existential.

John of the Cross himself refashions the traditional three stages of purgative, illuminative, and unitive in favor of dividing the dark night of the soul into two parts: The "dark night of sense" and the "dark night of the spirit." Both nights are afflictive, and the dark night of sense, especially pertinent to the neophyte, represents a weaning away from the sensual appetite. And this is, of course, an ascetic discipline. Asceticism, of which, no doubt, too much has been made in some of the spiritualities of the past, is, to be sure, out of fashion today—and this may be a reason why a real mysticism is also out of fashion. Asceticism, ironically, is itself sensual, and accordingly the great advocate of romantic love, Denis de Rougement, has observed how restraint *heightens* passion. Such an observation can be subversive in a consumer society. John, as we shall see, is himself no puritan, and his intent is to *purify* passion, not destroy it.

The dark night of sense might entail some special application in death and dying, where the problem can be less the denial of sense than the *presence* of sense. That is, the terrible problem of pain. If that, alas, should be one's lot, the thing obviously is less the denial of sense than its acceptance, ultimately, the acceptance of our "Cross." Suffering, before which mere language pales, will be taken up shortly. But John of the Cross does quote the text of Matthew (16:24): "If anyone would follow me, let him deny himself and take up his cross." Whatever our condition, we need not fabricate our Cross. It is usually at hand. But asceticism is not an end in itself, only a means to an end. Emptiness is a condition of fullness.

Read with circumspection, it is still essential to note that John knows, as it were, that spirit is not the opposite of sense. That is, the denial of the senses is no mechanical guarantee that one is becoming spiritual; progress in the first, the purgation of sense, can readily seduce us to regress in the second. That is, regress into self-complacency. Therefore, the purgation of "the dark night of sense" is followed by the even more taxing "dark night of the spirit", ("spirit" being the highest part of the soul). Here John would prune away pride, complacency, self-congratulation, and even desire for spiritual consolations. Such things can represent what he calls "sense overflowing into spirit," a *merely* natural spirituality. John's dynamic is a safeguard against our considerable capacity for self-delusory spiritual pride.

The watchword is detachment. John appropriates Jeremiah (23:26), noting that attachments can induce individuals to "see the visions of their heart" (*Ascent of Mount Carmel*, XXXI, 3). We are suggestible, including autosuggestible, and this text, it seems to me, helps account for the potential for ruinous and delusory "signs and wonders" so conspicuous in cults and uncritical spiritualities. That is, in any path not founded on the rock of radical honesty. John warns against measuring God by oneself, not oneself by God. "What is born of the flesh is flesh" (John 3:6), and John of the Cross would have us born of the Spirit. Accordingly, he would have us seek not the experience of God, but God. Preoccupation with the former can lead us to fall in love with our own feelings; unwittingly or not, in some sense, to worship ourselves. Therefore, with John, as I think with Paul, the experience of charity is not only the safest but the *highest* of religious experiences (1 Cor. 13).

But charity, one might protest, is likely to be *ordinary* experience. How "ordinary?" Truly, how ordinary? Charity is supernatural for, if history and human experience are any indicators—not to go into geniuses like Pascal, Kierkegaard, and Dostoyevsky—we are *naturally* egocentric. This is by no means to deny a higher nature, itself grace-given; Thomas Aquinas himself spoke of "sacraments of nature" and of a divine instinct (*instinctus divinus*) founded in the human condition. While John might appear to deny this, he really completes it. His mysticism, one might already surmise, is very pure, and one best undergoes purification before receiving it. One begins to be the recipient of this "mystical theology" in the dark night of the spirit, which is infused, secret, and passive. It is, if you will, "nocturnal," for it corresponds to "night." But John is not opposed to popularly construed "special" experiences (and more likely only "secondary effects") as such: Only to our *attachment* to them. Attachment engenders anxiety; detachment engenders peace. He recites the psalmist, "If riches abound, set not your heart on them" (62:10), or as one formula puts it, "Seek nothing, refuse nothing."

Negative theology accentuates detachment, the paradox of which John of the Cross enshrines in one of the most stunning passages of spiritual literature:

> In order to arrive at having pleasure in
>   everything,
> Desire to have pleasure in nothing.
>   In order to arrive at possessing everything,
> Desire to possess nothing.
>   In order to arrive at being everything,
> Desire to be nothing.
>   In order to arrive at knowing everything,
> Desire to know nothing.[7]

This refrain, an inspiration of T.S. Eliot's *Four Quartets,* is his effective equation of "nothing" (*nada*) and "everything" (*todo*), a coincidence of opposites that has its universal resonances. For example, in Zen, zero equals infinity. And with the paradox we see that John's austerity, at first so foreboding, is ultimately a *sensuous* austerity. This is above all evident in his poetry, a last great flowering of the venerable tradition of the Song of Songs. Let us listen to a little of his "night music":

> Let us rejoice, beloved,
> And go forth, reflecting each other in your beauty
> By mountains or below,
> Where purest waters flow,
> We'll pass deeper within the dark woods.[8]

I fancy this as an elopement scenario, and it is a song of mystical marriage and spiritual passage. The lover comes at night, without fanfare, ascends the mystical ladder, and gazes with joy upon his beloved. "Reflecting," I believe, can allude to Paul's great text: "And all we, with unveiled face, beholding the glory of the Lord, are being changed into his likeness." (2 Cor. 3:18). The Lover is, of course, God, whose union with the beloved, the soul, is emblematic of the mystery of divinization. Of this kind of mystery, the psalmist would sing: "Such knowledge is too wonderful for me" (139:6).

But it is not necessarily too mysterious for the Song of Songs. The Song of Songs is a venerable tradition in which human love can be raised, by analogy, to the level of the divine. That is, the ineffable is "encoded" in the more familiar idiom of symbolic language. We can recall the words of R. C. Zaehner, how "the raptures of the theistic mystics are closely akin to the transports of sexual union." Maurice Bezart, in an old program for "The Rite of Spring," put it inimitably: "Human love, in its physical aspect, symbolizes the same act by which God created the cosmos, and the joy that he drew from it." For John, restraint *has* heightened passion, as he weds the innocent and the erotic:

> Within my flower-like breasts,
> Which I keep for him alone
> My lover found his rest,
> And to him I gave my all
> Under cedar branches, gently blown.[9]

John can be playful, even androgynous, but his playfulness is "the liberty of the children of God." There is a "weightless" quality in his verse, which I believe exemplifies his thought that to renounce joy in particular things is to receive it in all things. John's faculties have been darkened or "cured." His three faculties of the soul—memory, understanding and will—correspond to the three theological virtues: "understanding" to faith, "memory" to hope, and "self-will" to charity. Faith voids but really "cures" understanding, raising it to wisdom; hope voids memory, evacuating, as Thomas Keating says, our "psychic debris," reorienting us from the "demons" of the past to the experience even now of the promise of things to come; and divine charity voids our endemic but ultimately fatuous self-will. This divinization of the faculties accounts for John's lightness of touch, as though he were no longer there. As though he might say, with Paul, "I live now not with my own life, but with the life of Christ" (Gal. 2:20). As though nothing *were* everything.

Interestingly, all this is from one who, in those "stunning" antitheses, forswears the pursuit of spiritual experience! John sought *God,* not his *experience* of God. And John is, ironically, as we can surmise from countless other texts, replete with spiritual experience. John renounces attachment and is supremely attached, i.e., divinely attached. For all this, the Mystical Doctor is not incoherent but simply inclusive, i.e., an unavowed embodiment of the coincidence of opposites. He trusted the invisible *light* through the *dark* night.

Let us conclude this consideration of St. John of the Cross with another personage who trusted, making a more familiar application of the mystery of night. The subject is that most benighted man of all, Job. The Book of Job is, of course, a parable, which is a way of saying that Job can be seen as living our life. Job was a just man, even prosperous, but in his good fortune did not enjoy the glories he longed for in his God. But when reduced to nothing, abandoned by his friends, naked on a dung-hill:

> then the Most High God, He that lifts up the poor man from the dung-hill, was pleased to come down and speak with him there face to face, revealing to him the depths and the heights of His wisdom, in a way that He had never done in the time of his prosperity.[10]

The Book of Job is really the "comedy" of God at the dung-hill. It dramatizes John's paradoxes of "nothing" and "everything."

The Cloud of Unknowing

If a survey of St. John of the Cross is taxing, though perfectly understandable, let us take comfort in *The Cloud of Unknowing*. This Middle English classic is not as intellectually demanding as John of the Cross. All the same, Evelyn Underhill herself hailed it as the foremost example of English mystical theology, an appreciation seconded on the other side of orthodoxy by Aldous Huxley. Though written several centuries earlier than John of the Cross, this anonymous treatise has been seen as an advance summary of John, and we shall review it to that end.

The Cloud of Unknowing, like John, is premised upon the darkness of God. God may be revealed as well as hidden, but the idea of the darkness of God, we might suggest, is as biblical as that of God-as-Light. In the awesome revelation of Sinai, God is hidden in a "dense cloud," and Sinai is "entirely wrapped in smoke" (Ex. 19:16–18). At the dedication of the temple, Solomon announced that "Yahweh has chosen to dwell in the thick cloud, and so thick was it that the priests could no longer perform their duties" (2 Chron. 5:14–6:1). "Darkness he made a veil to surround him" (2 Sam. 22:12). And He brought the Israelites out of Egypt "by night" (Deut. 16:1).

The author of *The Cloud*, as it is popularly called, simplifies (happily, perhaps wisely) our faculties to two: "Knowing" and "loving." But God, who dwells in this "dense cloud," is incomprehensible, and therefore cannot be comprehended by knowing. He is known (or "unknown") only by loving. Accordingly, we should detach ourselves from all other means, and direct a "naked intent" to God alone. "Covet not good things in particular," *The Cloud* says, "but only good God."[11] That is, as with John, "good things" are a function of "good God," not the reverse. The verse from Matthew (6: 33) "Seek you *first* the Kingdom of God," is analogous.

If his path is dark and narrow, the author of *The Cloud* is always discerning. He is fully aware of the violence implicit in emotionalism and irrationalism, and he even deems reason a "godlike thing."[12] To consolations he is indifferent. The problem with consolations, he affirms, is the disposition to make one'e love contingent upon them. Such a spirituality would represent an investment more than a commitment. A wiser psychologist than he might have known himself to be, he gently counsels "a cloud of forgetting." Like masters universally, he proceeds by disemcumbrance.

Exalted reason may be, but the thesis of our anonymous author is that the "the cloud of unknowing" can be penetrated only by "the sharp dart of longing love." Our whole life must be one of longing.

"Longing" is archetypal to human experience. Does not that word, so dear to St. Augustine ("We were made for Thee, O Lord, and weary is our heart until it rests in Thee"), express something primal and irreducible in our natures? Does it not envisage pilgrims of desire (there is a fine study, *The Pilgrimage of Desire*),[13] moving, ever onward, from satiation to satiation, insatiably? Still, as Augustine memorably observes, the pilgrimage is "not by steps, but by love," and by the purification of our loves. The author of *The Cloud* makes it clear that we could not love God unless God loved us first. Of that love he says, "Let it be active, and you passive."[14] Like John, the emphasis is upon enhancing receptivity. We receive by grace what cannot be acquired by nature. And the supreme grace, as the author of the *The Cloud* writes, is being "oned with God."

Negative Theology Reviewed

Let us first try to bring a few of these thoughts into better focus. First, if we are restricted to "unknowing," how do we *know*, as the *The Cloud* puts it, that we are "oned with God"? The question, of course, evokes discernment, not dogma, but we should note that the "unknowing" involves intellectual knowledge, whereas the problematic of being "oned" involves experiential knowledge. Certainly the latter, the question of spiritual union, is validated less by its "secondary effects," our subjective states, including the more oracular claims, than by our "works," that is, our life. St. John the Divine speaks to the point:

> We can be sure that we are in God only when the one who claims to be living in him is living the same kind of life that Christ lived (1 John 2:5–6).

Negatively put, "those who know do not talk," opens the *Tao Te Ching* , and "those who talk do not know." This is good negative theology. The real masters are generally rather mute about these things. Like Paul, when he relates his own experience of being "caught up into paradise," he only discloses that "he heard things that cannot be told, which man may not utter" (2 Cor. 12:4). One can suspect that he is speaking of something not so much morally forbidden as *verbally* impossible. A postulate of negative theology and, I believe, of mysticism generally, is that describable experience is inferior to indescribable experience. For example, an ostensible apparition of Christ is *unlikely* (not impossibly) describable as precisely "seven hundred feet." This does not deny that something of the experience cannot be communicated indirectly, especially through metaphor, symbol, and song. John of the Cross, as we have seen, turns in his ecstatic poetry to what may be the highest metaphor of them all, according to ancient traditions of both East and West, human and sexual love. Mysticism is in fact a mother of the arts. The Mystical Doctor, John, for example, is the eqivalent of the national poet of Spain, and at the other end of the world, Zen has nourished poetry, philosophy, and the fine arts generally.

Negative theology knows by unknowing, and its proponents stress, as it were, the importance of being ignorant. This ignorance stands for more than the intellectual "content" of kenotic self-emptying. Ignorance is the other side of "concentration"; in other words, it is positive. It stands as "ignorance" to the more conventional "wisdom of the world" or to mere conventional knowledge. It is ignorance to everything that is not God. Therefore, its ignorance is not imbecility but, to appropriate the title of Nicholas of Cusa, a "learned ignorance." I prefer to think of it as advanced or higher ignorance.

Negative theology delights in negatives, but finds in them something positive, though it may seem nothing to "the world." Therefore, we have recounted the irony of St. John of the Cross and his *nada*. But beneath the *no* of his nada looms an unspoken but more fundamental *yes*. The imperative here is not mere verbalization but what John Henry Newman calls "realisation."[15]

The author of *The Cloud of Unknowing* did as much justice to both verbalization and realization as we are likely to see in prose. I refer to his extraordinary and climactic book 68:

> "Nowhere" is where I want you! Why, when you are "nowhere" physically, you are "everywhere" spiritually. . . . Go on doing this no thing. . . . Who is then calling it "nothing"? Our outer self, to be sure, not our inner. Our inner self calls it "All."[16]

And "nowhere," to complete the irony, is now-here.

One of the greatest of our "holy fools" or holy "nihilists" (to speak foolishly) is Meister Eckhart. For Eckhart God is a "not-God." Or consider his *jocular* syllogism:

> I am good.
> 'God' is not 'good.' (God being incomparable)
> Therefore, I am better than God!

Luther's "scandalous" paradoxes can stretch language to its limits, literally making black white and white black:

> God's faithfulness and truth always must become a great "lie" before it becomes truth. . . . In short, God cannot be God unless he first becomes a "devil." We cannot go to heaven unless we first go to "hell."[17]

Small wonder Eckhart and Luther both had authority problems!

Negative theology is, if you will, a theology for "night persons"—and its votary one who, if you will, "sees in the dark." It is or is like:

> The sigh of the Psalmist: "In the night my heart instructs me" (16:7).

> The text "You will know the truth, and the truth will make you free" (John 8:32). This is a truth illuminated by the late Zen master, Katagiri Roshi, as "too close to us to know."

> "Passing over," to use that pregnant structure of John Dunne, *The Way of All the Earth*, from "knowing God" to knowing that we do *not* "know" God. And then maybe we do!

> Paul's "wisdom of the Cross" (1 Cor. 1:18–25).

> Eckhart's thought that God is what remains unsaid.

> The "secret" of the fox in *The Little Prince*: "It is only with the heart that one can see rightly; what is essential is invisible to the eye."

> The smile of the Cheshire cat.

> What is left after everything has been taken away.

> What is happening to us.

If negative theology has its dangers—but only when taken out of a more positive context—there may also be dangers in what is happening to us. For are we not all dying?

Prayer, Meditation, and Contemplation

Even prayer can be dangerous. Some of the early fathers intimated that when we enter prayer we cannot be sure that we shall come out of it alive. That is, we are not guaranteed survival if we pray with our whole being, surrender all control, empty ourselves before God—perhaps

empty ourselves too much. St. Teresa may have been un-
daunted by the challenge, in that she died in mystical
prayer. Hers was not the worst way of dying—and perhaps the most likely way to die in meditation is to *live* in
meditation.

But for most of us the "danger" of prayer is in the
other direction, that of blandness—of routinization.
Whatever the case, let it be said at the outset that the author is not a master of prayer but rather a plodding student of the masters.

Prayer, of course, is a generic and inclusive term and
can be submitted to various distinctions and subdivisions.
Some of the masters, for example, St. John of the Cross,
distinguish between "meditation" and "contemplation."
In this framework the latter is more advanced. "Meditation" can be systematic or spontaneous, private or communal, but it is what *we* do. But "contemplation,"
normally founded on meditation, is what *God* does. And
what God does *in us*. That is, contemplation is equivalent
to mystical or mysterious theology, and it is infused, secret, and passive. A kindly confessor once told me that in
prayer we speak to God, but in meditative reading, God
speaks to us. This is to suggest that meditation can "pass
over" into contemplation. Moreover, just as whatever God
has to say is presumably more important than anything
we have to say, contemplation is considered higher than
meditation. But the forms of prayer are like the traditional stages of spiritual development (purgative, illuminative, unitive) in that they can be experienced
simultaneously and are not necessarily sequential. The
main thing is that in entering the prayer life of the mystical fathers one need not relinquish the prayer life of the
child. When all is said and done, "of such is the kingdom
of heaven."

There is such a thing as a progression in prayer, a
matter of much discernment. Most of us are nurtured in
"discursive prayer," prayer as dialogue (or monologue),
which can loosely be included within meditation. St. John
of the Cross provides various signs for discerning if the
time is right to venture beyond this to a more inward si-

lence, as prelude to contemplation. One of these signs is that ordinary prayer and ordinary language often seem insufficient, even arid. Another is a felt need for more solitude. A third is a gnawing sense of the need to divest, to be unencumbered. These are among the pointers to the mystical path.

The forms of our prayer life, it seems to me, freely correspond to the forms of the heart's life. That is, the evolution of prayer would seem kindred to the human condition in what is likely to be its personal evolution of love. Accordingly, the language of young lovers is apt to be effusive, demonstrative, rhetorical, and of course delightful. As mature lovers, love is less something said than something done, and its language is likely to be filtered and patterned by the years, reduced to the tender essentials, regularly, all but ritually, repeated: "I love you." Or the expression of this kind of love can crystallize in the name of the beloved, endearingly repeated, as can happen in some of our most intimate moments. But old lovers may transcend even this, for whom it may be no more than shared glances, chaste listenings, gratitude, smiles, and silence. The first stage, with its conventional if heightened use of language, can correspond to discursive prayer; the second, more to systematic meditation—unconventional if not incantatory repetition of language; and the third, to contemplation—more translinguistic, mysterious, and diffused. Here *nothing* need be prayer for *everything* is prayer.

Certainly we should not insist that "systematic meditation" is essential to mystical experience. It was apparently not to Paul outside Damascus or to Stephen the martyr outside the walls of Jerusalem. God comes only through the awful grace of God. Prayer is not meant to control God but to liberate ourselves and, as a condition of liberation, to discipline ourselves. Bodily ecstasies and trance states, for example, are not necessarily a sign of higher spiritual gifts but of bodily, psychic, and perhaps even spiritual *weakness*. The psychospiritual system of the recipient might not have been grounded to withstand the divine charge, bespeaking a need for more systematic discipline. Spiritual fireworks, if you will, are considered by masters rather generally as rare for seasoned practitioners.

Prayer should be neither analyzed nor forced. Prayer can be many things: a response to beauty, a response to truth, a response to goodness. But where prayer is a response, it must first be a call.

Prayer can be a "calling." Monastics would understand instinctively. The notion of prayer as calling struck me in a special way when, some years ago, I was privileged to spend a semester at Tantur, a theological institute outside of Jerusalem. It was in the predominately Moslem area, culturally akin in so many respects to the age of the Bible itself, and as I explored the villages I could not but be fascinated with the wailing from the minarets of "the call to prayer." A haunting experience, this seemed to me, if one would but listen, an external expression of a more internal and subtle "call to prayer," as, for example, of the call of the One who "stands at the door and knocks." But we may not be disposed to hear this call unless lifted out of indifference by joy or fallen by circumstances into sorrow. Then out of the abundance of the one or the emptiness of the other, our "heart instructs" us (Ps. 16:7).

Prayer, then, is not "inauthentic." It is not "dualistic." It does not posit an authentic self menaced by an extrinsic and alien higher power. This reproach is a peculiar criticism occasionally advanced by partisans of one species of existentialism here or a strictly monistic spiritual tradition there. Of course, popular religion does incline to rather hard and fast categorization universally and *across* religious frontiers. That is, popular devotionalism universally is likely predicated of an objectification of God *here* and humankind *there*. While proponents of mystical theology assuredly enjoy no divine right to pretentions to hierarchy, as we shall intimate with several of our personal illustrations, it would seem time to move beyond mutually exclusive alternatives of either monism or dualism. Such constructions can themselves be categorical. Duality is a fact of experience, but prayer, especially deep prayer, attentuates if not dissolves duality. Prayer is not so much dualistic as it is, if you will, contrapuntal, "heart speaking to heart" (*Cor ad cor loquitur*), to appropriate the famous motto of Newman. Ultimately, as I shall suggest, there is only one Heart. We become what we worship; we become as intimately one as true lovers become one. And even more intimately, if, as R. C. Zaehner insisted, conjugal union is only the symbol of the higher reality.

Prayer should not be forced, but if we can believe Paul, it should be ceaseless. Prayer can be ceaseless if it becomes a state as well as an act. A resolution to the challenge of Paul is available to us in "The Prayer of the Heart." This is the famous "Jesus Prayer," one of the finest expositions of which is to be found in J. D. Salinger's *Franny and Zooey*. The full form of the prayer is usually rendered: "Lord Jesus Christ, Son of the living God, have mercy on me, a sinner." It is rooted in the "Prayer of the Publican" who, in contrast to the self-congratulation of the Pharisee, could not even lift his eyes to heaven, but beat his breast, repeating, "God, be merciful to me a sinner!" (Luke 18:13). It was enshrined in the Kyrie and evolved by the Desert Fathers. It simply varies familiar prayer formulas that many of us knew as children as an ejaculation. The idea, of course, is to repeat the prayer so incessantly and with such utter simplicity and naked intent that it becomes internalized and dissolves into the rhythms of the heart, as it were, beating it for us. *Here* is our "one Heart." Again, the Prayer of the Heart is kindred to our "call to prayer," where the caller and the pray-er become virtually indistinguishable. The intent of the prayer is to engender "a state," as we have suggested, a state of purity of heart: Spiritual transparency, instrumentality at the disposition of the Holy One. "The pure of heart," as the Master promised, "will see God" (Matt. 5:8).

This seeing of God may be fulfilled through death, but the Prayer of the Heart can suspend the boundaries between life and death. In its disarming simplicity, the prayer can fuse affectivity and intellection, illuminating the perennial theological imponderable concerning the human capacity for "seeing God." The pure of heart may see little else but God! That is to say, they can be endowed with God-consciousness, which is a state rather than an act.

Still, to some the Jesus Prayer, which has its universal variants, may be too long. It can of course be shortened, done contrapuntally as in the Kyrie—i.e., "Lord have mercy" alternating with "Christ have mercy—or reduced to one's own single word. One's personal and peculiar appropriation can evolve over time. Moreover, the "me" of the longer form may, for some, inhibit what St. John of the Cross called "holy oblivion." *The Cloud* speaks of "the cloud of forgetting." What might we remember if we forgot everything? St. Anthony of the Desert, the first Desert Father, counsels: "Perfect prayer is not to know that you are praying." Or as *The Cloud* says: " 'Nowhere' is where I want you."

Happily, *The Cloud of Unknowing* knows how to get there. That is to say, in monologic (one-word) meditation, the Western equivalent of the Eastern mantra. Let us quote from book seven of this remarkable work:

> If you want this intention [i.e., "a naked intention directed to God . . . alone"] summed up in a word, to retain it more easily, take a short word, preferably of one syllable, to do so. The shorter the word the better, being more like the working of the Spirit. A word like 'GOD' or 'LOVE.' Choose which you like, or perhaps some other, so long as it is of one syllable. And fix this word fast to your heart, so that it is always there come what may. It will be your shield and spear in peace and in war alike. With this word you will hammer the cloud and the darkness above you. With this word you will suppress all thought under the cloud of forgetting.[18]

In contemporary parlance, this is simply called meditation. Let us offer a practical aside. It is well enough

known that one should "practice" this word once or twice
daily, preferably at regular hours. If one should be a
"night person," a candle can be helpful, at least at the beginning, in facilitating concentration. A candle is a powerful symbol of "what is happening to us." This kind of
meditation quiets the body, suspends the mind, opens the
heart. The main thing, I think, is that one's word be said
slowly, gently, let fall "drop by drop upon the heart."
One's word can be timed with one's breathing so that in
time we do not say it as much as it "says us." At the beginning it can seem laborious, but we should remember
that prayer is really "play." That is, unlike "work," prayer
is an end in itself, from which any benefits, psychic or otherwise, are still only "secondary effects." Here again
prayer is like love. As St. Bernard said, "I love because I
love." We pray because we pray. It is its own "reason." It
is "right"—"meet and just," as in the formula of the
liturgy. Such prayer is relatively "undirected." That is, it
is not petitionary—it seeks only God's good pleasure.
Ironically, perhaps, undirected prayer can be more effi-
cacious than directed prayer, for it can bespeak greater
abandonment to the divine will. If it seems too alien, one
should of course stay with one's traditional prayer forms,
but monologic meditation is also useful as "pre-prayer."

What *The Cloud* alludes to is actually rooted in the
Desert Fathers and essentially known in the West today
as "the centering prayer." Its leading exponents today are
probably Thomas Keating and Basil Pennington, two distinguished, affable, and modest Cistercians. Their monologic prayer need not be monosyllabic. For example,
"Abba" ("Father," really "daddy") is a great favorite. With
them, one's "sacred word" is recited until, like a child run-
ning with a kite, the kite takes wind and lofts itself.
Therefore, the sacred word is used in tandem or alterna-
tion with contemplative silence. Advocates of the centering prayer would distance us, in our practice, from the
traditional "visual aids," images or icons (though I think
no one would deny their enduring value) and the exercise
of the imagination because the experience of God *exceeds*

the imagination. They would take us beyond every image or reflection for, as Fr. Keating[19] says, reflection is not a reality but a photograph of a reality. They can take us to, as the Angelic Doctor, St. Thomas, characterized prayer, "the simple enjoyment of the truth—in silence. And as Eckhart tells us, "In all the world there is nothing so much like God as stillness."[20]

Even gazing into the stillness can be prayer. The contemplative is visionary, given to gazing, rapt in a dark icon or a sunset. Nicholas of Cusa wrote a charming but very challenging meditation, *The Vision of God*, in which he contemplates "the gaze of God."[21] Eckhart spoke of prayer as looking at Him who is looking at me. For Eckhart, the eye with which we see God is the same eye with which God sees us.

Our very breath can be prayer, a most accessible way of praying ceaselessly. The Hebrew word for breath is the same as that for spirit, as in the Holy Spirit, *Ruah*. Breathing attentively can be the prayer of gratitude, especially breathing with a slight smile, the slightly illumined smile of gratitude. It is like the "sighs too deep for words" that Paul alludes to (Rom. 8:26), when the Spirit intercedes for us in our inadequacies and in the inadequacies of language. If the "bread believes," as poet James Carroll put it, we might add that the breath "believes." Prayer can be practice for death, and in death, as we exhale our last, we may be inhaled by God. That is, we may experience a species of "absorption."

With this, the counterpoint of prayer is harmonized into our song of St. Augustine. If all were silent, what would we hear? "Enter into Thy Master's joy."

"Be still, and know that I am God" (Ps. 46:10). But how do we know that a given experience is God? Ultimately, the proof is in the practice. But the experience of Elijah, the model of a mystic, may be helpful: "Yahweh was not in the wind. . . . Yahweh was not in the earthquake . . . but . . . in . . . the sound of a gentle breeze" (1 Kings 19:11–12). The experience of God is, generally, less like an earthquake than it is a simple awareness. An awareness of what one may have already "known," but for the first time savored. It can be like a "spiritual sense." This oxymoron, conventionally a coincidence of opposites, is a fascinating synthesis that descends to us from Gregory of Nyssa, a seminal thinker in negative theology. Any definition would adulterate it, but Gregory likens it to the "fragrance" that delights the bride in the Song of Songs. It is like love, and love always knows love.

"What you have come to is nothing known to the senses"—but we have, as it were, returned to our senses, after first having purified them, and a spiritual sense is enhanced, as St. John of the Cross writes, "a hundredfold."

We are not necessarily saving the "last rites" for last, but let us go no further without a few observations on the more or less traditional rites of passage, the sacramental life. Our concentration upon mystical prayer is by no means intended to slight the consolations of the sacraments, essential especially in the Catholic traditions. The author is himself nurtured and informed by these traditions.

And so too, it may be recalled was mysticism. Our very word *mysticism* is etymologically rooted in the early Christian "Mysteries," i.e., sacraments. Like a good song, the archaic or noumenous power of the sacraments can suffer from exposure and routinization, itself a reason for an antidotal negative theology. The sacraments not only "render present," but can suggest how much is reserved *behind* the ordinariness of their "sign" or "form," elemental things like water, bread, and wine. These elements can suggest how, covertly, the "world is charged with the grandeur of God" (Gerard Manley Hopkins).

The sacraments continue to have mystical import. In the context of death and dying, the last rites come naturally to mind. But one need not await that. It happens that one of the finest insights and kindest compliments on the Eucharist that I have ever heard came from the venerable Zen master, Thich Nhat Hanh. Speaking in a Berkeley church several years ago, he simply observed that Christians were fortunate to have the sacrament of the Eucharist, for it was a powerful symbol of Buddhist "mindfulness." Sitting before the sacrament of the altar can be, for many, an incomparable focus for quiet meditation. After all, what is contemplation (*cum templo*) but in some root sense to be in the temple, before "the holy of holies," presence to Presence. And the Eucharist is linked unambiguously with the promise of resurrection and life eternal (John 6:51–54). The "Mystery" belongs most vitally to mysticism, death and dying.

"Yes"

Let us conclude our meditation on negative theology with, if you will, an affirmation. The word is "yes." After all, the devil, not the puritan, is the first "nay-sayer." Goethe's Mephistopheles identifies himself: "I am the spirit that denies." And what is so much merely human history, as distinguished from a mysteriously divine history in which it is mixed, but a commentary upon and echo of the primal *non serviam*—"I will not serve"? Humbly monosyllabic, the monologic yes (in which we are told, interestingly, the Hindu word *OM* is rooted), is, I venture, the most revolutionary word in our history. Women might understand it best; certainly, one woman did. As St. Bernard of Clairvaux, in his celebrated sermons on the Madonna-to-be, sermons, which made all the world first fall in love with the eternal feminine, swells in song: "All heaven and earth await your 'yes,' Oh Virgin!" She answered yes: "Be it done to me according to thy word."

The word *yes* can be the most revolutionary word in *our* history. And it can be the most revolutionary word at the end of our own personal history. This at least is the belief of Ladislaus Boros in his very suggestive book, *The Moment of Truth: Mysterium Mortis*.[22] Rarely has a book more direct application to the potential affinity, even syncronicity, of prayer and death.

The book of Boros is premised upon the unconditional love of an all-merciful God. He goes even beyond Søren Kierkegaard, who held that true conversion is only at "the eleventh hour," a thought likely to be compatible with the experience of our own inveterate vacillation and, as often turns out, premature commitment. Boros goes beyond "the eleventh hour" to, as it were, midnight, the nocturnal hour, as the moment of truth. That is, at the moment of death, everyone, whether virtuous or not, believer or not, is confronted with the loving gaze of Christ and the "final decision." Death has rarely been more mystical. But at this moment of supreme concentration we must choose, and with the whole of our being. The application is literal:

> By his Yes or No man finally passes judgement on himself. . . . Whoever utters in death the Yes of his life is not condemned. But whoever says "No" to Christ's love has already condemned himself. . . . He chooses himself for ever: he must therefore endure himself eternally.[23]

Hell, in the view of Boros, is not "other people" (as Sartre believed) but self, and it is essentially a product of having rejected an all-encompassing love. It might be wise to start practicing now. Yes!

The Prayer of Suffering, or Purgatory on Earth: St. Thérèse and Etty Hillesum

Suffering is, or can be, the highest form of prayer. This seems to me a comfort in a culture where the sick are apt to be shut away as useless and superfluous, or where we are almost daily "anesthetized" to death—not, of course, that there is no need for clinical anesthetics. Moreover, some spiritual masters may stress too much that prayer best requires a composed spirit. Prayer is, as William McNamara says, "a cry of the heart," and it is best to let the heart sob itself out. It goes without saying that we prefer to pray at a safe distance from any human torment, but we may be called, like Christ, to make our descent into hell. I prefer to think of it as purgatory on earth.

We have considered night as faith and night as God, including the divine flowing into our lives, but there is no way around our third meaning of the term: affliction. In popular terms, this may constitute the *entire* meaning of "the dark night of the soul."

Let us review and specify some of our earlier reflections on suffering. Philosophically speaking, we should avoid either pessimism or optimism. And here I follow Friedrich von Hügel, *The Mystical Element of Religion*,[24] considered by people like Evelyn Underhill and Morton Kelsey to be the greatest study of mysticism of our century in the English language. Von Hügel counsels against the polarities of pessimism and optimism: on the one hand, a morbid pessimism that sees only suffering but denies the reality of the world as an escape, and on the other hand, a superficial and illusory optimism that sees only a romanticized world as "moonlight and roses" and denies or rationalizes the reality of suffering. The latter "sees no evil," the former nothing but. Both solutions are too magical, smack of sleight-of-hand, and are ultimately unworthy of the subject. They incline toward a religious philosophy of Stoicism and its variants, whose object is apathy, denies the whole range of human emotion and passion, and throws out the baby with the bath. Both are really unhuman.

A spirituality that denies our humanity denies the Cross. And if we take the crucifixion seriously we acknowledge that suffering is the highest form of love and can be, to use our old theological term, redemptive. This is not just the view of traditional Christianity but also that of a radical death-of-God theologian like Dorothy Soelle, *Suffering*, or a Jewish psychiatrist like the sagacious Viktor Frankl, *The Doctor and the Soul*. Frankl, who as a survivor of the Holocaust ought to know, insists that there is meaning in suffering, and that it inoculates us against apathy and "psychic *rigor mortis*."[25]

Suffering, then, is simply a fact of human existence. It is also a bond of human existence. It makes for sensitivity, compassion and solidarity—including communion universally with the biblical "the halt, the lame, and the blind." There is a communion of suffering, just as there is "the communion of saints." We should not court suffering, but confront it, putting it to work for us rather than against us. The difference between the two, for or against, is not in the suffering as much as in the intention we associate with it. Of this, Abbot Chapman wisely observed, "We suffer best when we resent and hate the suffering, and *feel we are bearing it badly*."[26]

Like mysticism, then, suffering is a great paradox. The acceptance of suffering can somehow mitigate it. Acceptance of suffering, no matter how absurd the suffering *and* the acceptance of it may seem to be, means somehow that the world makes sense. We shall specify theologically in our last chapter why it is that our attitude toward suffering is significant. However apparently absurd, suffering *means*. It means that nothing is, ultimately, vain; that suicide is not the recourse of the wise; that Auschwitz, even Auschwitz, is not the last stop. In short, if we would let it, it means that good comes out of evil (Gen. 50:20, Rom. 8:28). But this does not make that evil good. Again, in our letting go of hope, hope can mysteriously enter, but it is no longer *our* hope. It is an infused theological virtue. Our security is in the surrender of *our* security. But the supreme paradox is how we can be healed by our wounds, even though we may not be healed the way we expected to be healed. As it is said, "God writes straight with crooked lines." The whole rhythm of spirituality is summed up in the ancient *O felix culpa*: From the "happy fault" of the Fall to the foot of the Cross and Resurrection. "Oh happy chance," runs a refrain of St. John of the Cross. Suffering, then, is a mystery, and there is such a thing as "the sacrament of suffering," "a visible sign of invisible grace." It is a rite of passage, perhaps our final rite of passage.

The associations of mysticism and suffering are perennial, even inevitable. Our mysticism was forged in the desert, with the Burning Bush, the Exodus experience, and the Desert Fathers, and is likely to rise from the ashes of our own individual "desert experiences." The very blood of Christ "urges" it on. I muse that there must be a "mystic" correspondence between Paul's being thrice "shipwrecked" (2 Cor. 11:25)—an apt metaphor for much of the human condition—and his account of being lifted to the "third heaven" in the subsequent chapter of the same letter (12:2). Paul's shipwreck echoes, across the centuries. For example, Jay Baldwin, a San Francisco nurse stricken with AIDS, volunteered:

> I never thought of AIDS as a gift from God. But it can really help one to come to terms with their spirituality. It's the normal inclination to put things on hold, but when you've got AIDS, you know you can't. (*San Francisco Examiner*, 3 May, 1987)

There are larger variants of this peculiar "logic" of the spirit. The paradox is operative in macrohistory as well as microhistory—in world history as well as personal history. It is no accident, I submit, that the fourteenth is sometimes considered the worst century—with its Black Death, Hundred Years War, and economic, civil, and ecclesiastical chaos. It is also one of the most creative centuries in the history of mysticism. Our own century may well rival the fourteenth in terms of human agony and, happily, may augur compensating promise in terms of the Spirit. Good comes out of evil, if we would let it.

This does not appear to be the case when sorrow first speaks, and it could be advanced that there are more economic ways of producing good. Well, God works with what God is given. At least *someone* honors human freedom. Much of our suffering, in short, is simply a contingency of our freedom.

The author recognizes how hollow and possibly even irritating some of this may sound to one to whom sorrow has spoken, but his purpose is not so much to analyze as to illustrate. And he is also shameless enough to turn to the putative "weaker sex" for his illustrations. He did not seek them: They were simply there. Let us attempt to illuminate purgatory on earth with several sketches here, plus several in our final chapter.

Women seem to have a special vulnerability to suffering. This is not a philosophical but a historical statement. That is, it is not a program but a fact. Women may not understand suffering any more than men, but they have certainly experienced it. Interestingly, most of the Western mystics may have been women. For example, of the 321 stigmatics recognized by the Catholic Church, only forty-seven are men.[27] This may have something to do with "the wound of love." It may represent a broader application of that seminally feminine text, "When a woman is in labor . . . " (John 16:21), amplified. What man might say, with Simone Weil, "Every time that I think of the crucifixion of Christ, I commit the sin of envy"?[28] This might strike us as a little hyperbolic, but those who knew her never questioned that she meant it. Apparently so deeply ingrained is some correspondence between women and suffering that Paula Caplan published *The Myth of Women's Masochism* (1985) to demonstrate that women are not inherently masochistic. Moreover, mysticism *is* considered "feminine" in that we are its passive recipients (and passive, passion, and suffering are all of an etymological family). Mysticism is even "bridal," in that its highest state is the bride of "mystical marriage."

Let us proceed with two unlikely parallel lives, St. Thérèse of Lisieux (1873–97) and our saint of the Holocaust, Etty Hillesum (1914–43). One was a French Catholic, steeped in traditional piety; the other, a secular Dutch Jew. One ingenuous, the other sophisticated, but both were spontaneous, vivacious, and compassionate. They both suffered poor health and died as young women, respectively at twenty-four and twenty-nine. And they were both, as it were, anointed for suffering.

St. Thérèse, "the Little Flower," is one of the most popular saints of the century, but she was completely unsung in her own time. Her life was ordinary enough. Impetuous—or perhaps she knew something that we do not—she entered the Carmelite cloister at fifteen, and died there less than ten years later. We know her best for her "little way,"[29] a still earlier tradition once called "the

spirit of childlikeness": "the alms of smiling," as she inimitably put it. It subsists in things like the laundry done
with love—not so much ascending Mount Carmel as get-
ting off one's high horse.

It would be easy to exaggerate the naïve charm of
Thérèse, to take as text a line from her very first letter, at
age four: "I'm a little imp, always laughing," as she
boasted of playing "naughty tricks" on her sisters."[30] That
does not express *The Hidden Face*, the title of Ida Fredericke Görres's life of St. Thérèse, surely one of the finest
studies of a saint ever done. True, when she was informed
of the onset of tuberculosis, some two years before the
end, she greeted the news with astonishing joy: An early
invitation to be with her beloved.

But first she had to be tried by fire. Morphine was de-
nied her, intestinal gangrene set in, and her agony became intolerable. Her winsome countenance still
prevailed, but there were hints of a descent into hell. John
of the Cross described the dark night of the soul as "a war
in the soul," of "contraries against contraries." "When this
pure light assails the soul," he writes, "in order to expel
its impurity, the soul feels itself so impure and miserable
that it believes God to be against it, and thinks that it has
set itself against God" (II, v, 5). "Impurity" may be pretty
hard to detect in Thérèse, but it should be measured not
against self but against "this pure light" into which the
self is being transfigured. In all events, Thérèse was be-
set by vicious temptations. She felt herself damned and
clawed at by the mockery of devils. Inauspicious in saints,
she confided: "I no longer believe in eternal life . . . only
love remains."[31]

But *her* love was eternal, and she resolved her suffering by letting it pass through her. She resolved it by fidelity to her own earlier resolution: "I offer myself as a
holocaust." And finally, she resolved it by fidelity to her
own "little way": "Little children are not damned."

Thérèse was a *woman* and a saint. If the sweetness
of her late romantic piety is out of fashion now, she will
always be an inspiration to truly sensitive souls. Her
most famous saying, I think, is not that she would send

us flowers from heaven, but her own unequivocal and supremely tough-minded: "All is grace." To Thérèse, this even included an apparent descent into hell.

One of Thérèse's flowers may have been Etty (Esther) Hillesum. Like Thérèse, Etty had an interrupted life, the title of her testament or diary, which has already been acclaimed by one reviewer as "the most spiritually significant document of our age." Yes, and it may prove among the most significant of any age.

Etty Hillesum seemed an unlikely saint. A student who stayed on at Amsterdam, in a somewhat communal existence, she may sound like a child of the 1960s. She was a "liberated woman" who became a fully liberated woman, a "free spirit" who became a truly free spirit. That is, she progressed to "the glorious liberty of the children of God" (Rom. 8:21). On the first page of her diary, one of the most remarkable documents of our time, she confides, "I am accomplished in bed." Her last entry, less than two years later, concludes: "We should be willing to act as a balm for all wounds."[32] This alludes to a spiritual revolution.

How might we account for the difference? First, Etty may be one of those rare souls who is "naturally good." But she follows nature to its source, where it becomes more than mere nature. This I think her sexuality evidences. To enlarge upon our opening quote: "I am accomplished in bed . . . and love does indeed suit me to perfection, and yet it remains a mere trifle, . . . and deep inside me something is still locked away." Love did indeed suit her to perfection, and she began to perfect it, uncovering that something "still locked away." Later she confesses and corroborates: "My passion used to be nothing but a desperate clinging to—to what, exactly? To something that one cannot cling to with the body."[33] In other words, her love-life literally embodies an unconscious hidden agenda, as it were, and is gradually raised from the human to the divine.

Etty "loved much." I think of the words of Gregory the Great that, with conversion, what had been the source of our vice can become transfigured into the source of our virtue. Or the thought of Gregory Palamas, of the Eastern Church, that the flesh can be a source of unimaginable sanctification. This means, as over against some presumptions about dualism, that the flesh not only embodies but itself *is* another great mystery. That is, it is not without paradox. It seems that if an over-weening human spirit doubts, there is something in the flesh, like the "bread", that "believes." Even our most intimate moments are not an alternative to, but an expression of, paradox. Sexual insatiability intimates horizons that transcend sex. The greater sins such as pride are "spiritual," not fleshly. This is a reason that St. John of the Cross followed the pruning of "the dark night of sense" with the even more demanding pruning of the "dark night of the spirit." In sum, the spirit is not the opposite of the flesh. Again, Etty was endowed with great freedom of spirit, and it is reassuring to see someone exercise that freedom creatively, not destructively, and to follow it to its logical, spiritual conclusion. At no point did the free spirit issue some "so far and no farther." Etty went truly "all the way."

Of course, there were many other reasons for the change, which was no doubt rendered more urgent by the ever-enveloping spectre of Nazism. She resolved, as she put it, to cease living "an accidental life." One can observe her reading going beyond Rilke, a great favorite, and Tolstoy and Dostoyevsky to Kierkegaard, St. Augustine, and the Bible, including the New Testament. She assimilates Christian spirituality, without of course sacrificing her Jewish identity, and quotes the Gospel with great reverence. This too is a part of her freedom. She even at times thinks of herself as a nun. She even has a kind of "rule":

To be very inobtrusive, and very insignificant, always striving for greater simplicity . . . don't try too hard to be interesting, keep your distance, be honest, fight the desire to be thought fascinating to the outside world.[34]

Interestingly, Etty's phrases "very inobtrusive" and "very insignificant" sound like a reincarnation of Thérèse's "little way."

A turning point for Etty is undoubtedly her turn inward. Contrary to her accustomed disposition, she begins to meditate in the morning, so to speak, to see if anything is there. Prayer could not be more authentic, even in its body language. Some feminist theologians even speculate today that a woman's *body* is her "spiritual director."[35] Let us let Etty speak for herself and of her call to prayer:

> A desire to kneel down sometimes pulses through my body, or rather it is as if my body has been meant and made for the act of kneeling. Sometimes, in moments of deep gratitude, kneeling down becomes an overwhelming urge, head deeply bowed, hands before my face.
>
> It has become a gesture embedded in my body.[36]

Etty seems to incarnate the idea of Gregory of Palamas—of the flesh as an unimaginable source or sanctification.

Etty is not only naturally good, but naturally theological, though formally untheological. That is, it is remarkable how sound, how deep, is her theological sense. She is inclusive or dialectical by nature: That is, hers was the inclusive both/and as opposed to the exclusive either/or. For example, she knew that God is *both* immanent *and* transcendent; not only the deepest but also the highest, both within *and* without. Most subtly, she knew that life and death are ultimately inseparable, that one cannot be fully alive unless one is partially "dead." As she put it: "It sounds paradoxical: by excluding death from our life we cannot live a full life, and by admitting death in our life we enlarge and enrich it."[37] God was "within," but equally within *others*, and she drew the maximum ethical conclusion from this. She could not hate. She could not even hate the Nazis, however they may have sullied or perverted their own divine image.

Still, Etty suffered absolutely no illusions about the Nazis or her prospects: "The lice will be eating me up in

Poland before long." To the numbness and despair of the
transit camp at Westerbork, she is the presence of hope.
She functions like a Mother Teresa, tirelessly comforting
the elderly and the infirm, bathing infants, passing along
meager rations, and all with, as Thérèse put it, "the alms
of smiling." And this at a time when her own health was
precarious. For her, suffering was not a philosophical
problem but a way of life, and she never doubted for a moment that "real suffering is always fruitful and can turn
life into a precious thing." And that is what it did to this
lovely woman, whose suffering ended at Auschwitz, on
30 November, 1943. Small wonder that, with her aboard,
she could write in a last chance postcard en route, "We left
the camp singing."

Like all saints, Etty had a secret. But a secret accessible to all: "The flesh is an unimaginable source of sanctification." She had an extraordinary capacity for love,
which is an extraordinary capacity for God. This brought
her to the miracle of not only accepting her fate, but being grateful for it: Seeking nothing, refusing nothing, loving everything. Only a mystic infused with a wisdom that
surpasses human understanding, and sometimes even of-
fends it, could write:

> When one has reached the point of experiencing
> life as something significant and beautiful, even in
> these times, or rather precisely in these times, then
> it is as if everything that happens has to happen just
> as it does and in no other way.

Or again:

> And yet, God, I am grateful for everything. I shall
> live on with that part of the dead that lives forever,
> and I shall rekindle into life that of the living which
> is now dead, until there is nothing but life, one great
> life, oh God.[38]

This sounds like another promise of a bouquet of
"flowers from heaven." Etty may not be much compensa-
tion for the Holocaust, but she may be a beginning.

Neither Etty nor Thérèse was theological, but they came to know, sure as master Friedrich von Hügel, that suffering can be "the highest form of action."[39] I think Etty and Thérèse would have liked each other. I believe that they do.

If Etty and Thérèse are still too remote and out of reach—too close to Paul's own "I rejoice in my sufferings for your sake" (Col. 1:24)—let me indulge in a personal memory. It is only a minor miracle, and I think of it as Aunt Doo's last ordeal. Her final ordeal was not to die but to live. My aunt was a saint of the family, completely self-giving, and her robust health was shattered toward the end by a series of strokes. Her frame increasingly skeletal, she wasted away in a nursing home, often in her own waste. That a grand but simple lady should be reduced to this ignominy? Her spirit could oscillate between resigned sufferance and rebellion with a despairing curse. This too can be only a way of sobbing oneself out, and a curse can somehow become a prayer. But prayer was her natural discourse, and at times she could be found alone in her room, wailing out her touching old evangelical hymns. Useless? I went to comfort her, but she was really inspiring me. I never doubted that she was destined for and delivered unto glory. After she died, I was accompanied to the funeral home by my five-year-old niece. I lifted Lee Lee, as we called her then, so that she might pay a last homage at the coffin. As only a child might, she spontaneously exclaimed: "She looks just like Jesus." And she did.

The Night is the Time of Salvation

We have come some distance from, but I think, with, our gallant teenager Burlena Turner and her dread of the night. We have seen such dread as something of a universal disposition, though culturally reinforced and psychologically conditioned. Night seems evocative of an older title of Ingmar Bergman, *The Hour of the Wolf.* We have advanced some means of deconditioning and re-

visioning our fear of night—night whether as physical reality or metaphor for the misfortunes inherent in the human condition—by our recourse to negative theology. We
have also had recourse to that veritable nightingale of the
spirit, St. John of the Cross, who could sing so sweetly in
the night:

> Oh night, you were my guide!
> Oh darkness, lovelier than the dawn!
> Oh night, that joined the beloved and her lover,
> Transforming the one into the other.[40]

John's verse, we can be reminded, was not the product of
some ivory tower but of imprisonment under the most
squalid and demeaning circumstances. Interestingly, imprisonment for a period of nine months, a powerful symbol of gestation. For John, the darkness was an excess of
light. He held to the Real Presence behind the apparent
absence.

This is, of course, no easy thing to do. And we might
well, with the psalmist (142:2), also pour out our com-
plaint.

Recently, the author returned to Toledo, site of
John's imprisonment where, at evensong, he chanced to
hear from the breviary "a little night music" that might
do justice to John. The refrain was, "The night is the time
of salvation." Let the author translate, with some free
adaptations, and let the reader continue with his or her
own adaptations as he or she might please:

> The night does not interrupt
> Your history with humankind.
>
> The night is the time of salvation.
>
> At night You descend Your mysterious stairway,
> On the same stone where Jacob slept.
>
> The night is the time of salvation.
>
> At night You celebrate Passover with your people,
> In darkness they escape from the bondage of Egypt.

The night is the time of salvation.

The stars of night are as the descendants of
Abraham,
Proof of Your promises, calming all creation.

The night is the time of salvation.

At night, three times did you call Samuel by
name,
Dreams were long Your most profound language.

The night is the time of salvation.

The night was witness of Christ in the tomb,
The night saw the glory of his resurrection.

The night is the time of salvation.

By night, we await the return of the bridegroom,
You will see at a glance the light of our lamps.

The night is the time of salvation.

Let us conclude our chapter of nocturne with premonitions of "dawn" and a paradox that sums up negative theology at a stroke. In the words of Clement of Alexandria, an early church father and observer: "All is unfailing light, and the place of the setting sun has become the place of its rising."[41]

This is almost enough to make us love the night.

3

Immolation: The Sacrifice

Try, then, to imitate God, as children of his that he loves, and follow Christ by loving as he loved you, giving himself up in our place as a fragrant offering and a sacrifice to God.

—Eph. 5:1–2

My God, my God, thou hast made this sick bed thine altar and I have no other sacrifice to offer but myself.

—John Donne, *Devotions*

Prefatory

This is a chapter on love. And, at least for those who have "put away the things of a child," sooner or later love is sacrificial.

I cannot but recall a rather too conspicuous chapter in the annals of love of some twenty-five years ago. In fact, as I write, Public Radio has been announcing that this is the anniversary of the release of the Beatles's *Sergeant Pepper's Lonely Hearts Club Band* (1967), the anthem of a generation that was going to turn the world around with love. A San Francisco underground paper *The Oracle* was proclaiming "the City of God," St. Augustine's great symbol. And there were reportedly sightings of Christ all over California. Like many, I was fascinated with the apparition of the flower children: cult or apocalypse? Though more sympathetic than not, I was rather quizzical as to whether these were "flowers" bestowed by Therésè or Etty. They could have been, at the beginning, but flowers require roots and cultivation.

Pursuing scholarly research, I traveled widely that summer, but it was coincidentally my own pilgrimage of love, pondering, "What is *this* thing called love?" When I chanced upon a curious sign in a window of what were then called headshops in Venice, California, advertising "INSENSE," I knew that this was no apocalypse. When I chatted with—interviewed is too formal a term— exotically beaded and painted flower children in Trafalgar Square only to discover that they did not distinguish between love and lust, I knew that "the summer of love" would be just that: a summer. We would have to look elsewhere. Fortunately, I chanced upon the answer to the question of that old refrain, but it was rather remote from the habitats of the flower children. It was in the great cathedral of Toledo, in Spain. There I saw, or thought I saw, an inscription on the main altar: *AMOR SACERDOS IMMOLAT* ("love immolates the priest"). Love as immolation. I sensed immediately that *this* was that thing called love. Not "insense," but incense. Paul himself expressed it with such marvelous economy: "A fragrant offering and a sacrifice to God." But incense, if you will; going up in smoke.

The inscription was on the altar, and the altar is a place of sacrifice. The priest is the one who makes the sacrifice, but there is a deeper sense in which the priest *is* the sacrifice. And if we can believe Peter, in some sense we are *all* priests. As they say, we should be careful what we pray for, for we might get it.

"Incense"? Harsh perhaps, but we will all be ashes one way or the other. Note the kindness with which Paul introduces his text: "*Try*, then to imitate God," reassuring us, "as children of his that he loves, and follow Christ." This gets us back to the essentials of a "positive theology," for God is not just hidden but revealed. Sooner or later there has to be more than "night," more than "nothing." There must be a revelation of love incarnate: Of a mysterious love, greater than death. Paul has here again, in a single sentence, given us a synopsis of mystical theology: Of "loving the way God loves." He invites us to "try." Shall we?

The Sacrifice

Sacrifice is the oldest religious institution known to humankind. Though it may appear out of fashion in a consumer society, there is no reason to suppose that it will disappear. Since sacrifice is found universally, in all religious cultures, it must express something elemental in human nature. We are not just, as Aristotle says, rational animals, but also sacrificial animals. For example, the insight has been advanced that, if there is not an adequate outlet for the sacrificial in contemporary culture, there are idealistic or sacrificial individuals who will pursue it in cults, including perverse cults, as well as political variants. This can eventuate in new applications of the old Roman adage: The worst are a corruption of the best.

The historic origins of ritual sacrifice are shrouded in a certain obscurity. With the pagan nations, rites of sacrifice were more or less magical or mechanical things, intended to appease the gods, control them, or bring down their power. The sacrificial victim could be animal or human. With the ancient Israelites, there was a gradual purification or progression, with an eventual call for a "sacrifice of the heart" (e.g., Hos. 6:6). Nevertheless, sacrificial rites were to be performed morning and evening. It was an expression of gratitude, petition, expiation, and communion.

Now it stares us in the face again, the ancient "evening sacrifice." Our intention, then, is not to review ancient history, but to explore immediate application. Let us proceed by offering several seemingly unconventional perspectives, one communal, taking its lead from the last word of the previous paragraph, and one historical, illuminating the farther reaches of rueful human sacrifice, directing us eventually to the center of the Christian mystery.

First, let us contemplate the communal. Philippe Ariès, in his various fine studies,[1] reminds us that centuries ago death was a communal and even public experience. It was a social fact, with kith and kin, even strangers from the street, gathered around. The bell tolled for everyone. While this larger family kept vigil in prayer, the expiring one would in turn dispense his last counsels, admonitions, and blessings and, in turn, receive the balm of the last rites. This kind of communal and sacramental support has too often been lost with the transiency, anonymity, secularity, and alienation of modern life. We are captive to our myth of illusory autonomy, and nowadays we are more likely to die alone, monitored only by the latest medical technology, unless we are blessed enough to have a few loved ones in attendance. Death is devoid of a public meaning and increasingly—or inevitably—a private meaning. The secular variety of existentialism has simply brought this to its logical conclusion in declaring death absurd.

This need not be. In principle, it *cannot* be. Paul bespeaks a universal truth: "The life and death of each of us has its influence on others" (Rom. 14:7). This influence should be maximal and optimal, and it can be if we make of our life and death, our life-in-death, a sacrifice.

Among the most insightful words I have seen on the subject are those of Martin Foss:

> The absurdity of death lies not only in its chance character, but also in its supposed isolation, which renders it meaningless, shutting it off from anything before and after. Sacrifice, as which alone death can be experienced, is the very opposite of this empty and isolated fact; it is devotion, reaching out in giving, and thus it is the most sublime bond which links life with life.[2]

Foss is saying that sacrifice establishes communion, a word with its various levels of meaning, and death becomes our last sacrament.

Our culture is antiheroic: Conformist, consumerist, and opiatic. If we cannot live dangerously, this is an invitation to die "dangerously." To cease living, as Etty Hillesum put it, "an accidental life." To act, not react. To discover or rediscover both our authentic identities as capacities for God and our common destiny, a transcendent destiny that triumphs over every absurdity. As against absurdity, sacrifice establishes meaning, and as against estrangement, sacrifice de-alienates death.

Death dissociates, sacrifice associates. That is, death sunders connections, but sacrifice, as Martin Foss put it, is "the very opposite," establishing "the most sublime bond which links life with life." It bonds more than life with life. As over against angst of isolation in space and contraction in time, in one's darkest night, sacrifice can associate us with "the evening sacrifice" of the ancient Israelites. Sacrifice not only roots us, it accesses "last things"—a realized eschatology—i.e., it associates us with the only community that has a real future, the communion of saints. Sacrifice not only de-alienates death, it universalizes life. It *means*.

The key to this universality—among other things an equation of "nowhere" and "everywhere" in *The Cloud of Unknowing*—is in what its author calls "naked intent." That is, as John Donne prayed, intent makes "this sick bed thine altar."

The mystical logic of sacrifice can be enlarged by our second and complementary perspective. Sacrifice is not only the oldest institution in history: In some sense it is the substance of history. But here we admit the demonic into our reflections, and the demonic is not the stuff of horror movies any more than mysticism is the stuff of the occult. With our sanguinary history, we do not need horror movies!

We allude to *human* sacrifice and an argument advanced in another book.[3] There is a wise French proverb: "Happy people have no history," and a great scholar,

Mircea Eliade, has written of "the terror of history." And rightly so, for what is history, when all is said and done but the conflict of good and evil? With the primitive, "the terror of history" seems to find its most dismal and maximal symbol in the universal practice of human sacrifice. We need not tax the reader with statistics, recite cases from even those most sophisticated of the ancients, the Greeks, or remind the reader that this practice still occurs here and there, and not just among preliterate societies. But what is human sacrifice but the ultimate expression, if you will, of the "natural right" of "the strong" to inherit the earth? We allude, ironically, to the triumph of *lower* amoral nature. And this anomaly encapsulates the movement and substance of history.

Of course, the author is aware that history is not just predatory but consists of a countervailing divine history, a movement of recovery, reconciliation, reintegration. But he is here speaking of history as that which shattered the harmony of paradise, flows not from the creation as from the Fall, and everywhere bears its mark. If this kind of language should sound credulous to some, the dehumanizing sign of the Fall is empirical and demonstrable. The sign of the beast is conspicuous, for example, in "the human sacrifice" of the Holocaust. And if the Holocaust was not essentially *human* sacrifice, what? Our gods are whatever we sacrifice to—be it the nation-state, the market, or only the imperious ego—our victims are whatever we sacrifice. As Carl Jung maintained, the old gods have not died: They have only changed their names. History repeats itself but not without a disarming change of costume.

In sum, history is about human sacrifice, and the antidote to human sacrifice is *divine* sacrifice. The cure, as it were, a species of homeopathic medicine ("like cures like"), is commensurate with the illness. Divine sacrifice is a self-giving sacrifice that reverses the flow of Eliade's "terror of history" and the psalmist's (91:5) "the terrors of the night." A sacrificial death, in this perspective, throws us into the breech of all history and the struggle with its "principalities and powers" (Eph. 6:12). This de-alienating death could hardly be more heavily pregnant with meaning. History inaugurates death, and "the last thing to be conquered is death" (1 Cor. 15:26). A sacrificial death means that this is not the end of our history, but its perpetuity in a self-transcending movement to end history, dissolved into everlasting glory.

Our Sacrifice and the Sacrifice of Christ

We have arrived at last at Unamuno's "the eternalizing, the deifying, the religious Christ."[4] His "religious Christ" transcends the mere "moralist" of modern secular culture. For his Christ is not just a philosopher of life but a conqueror of death.

Sacrifice associates, and divine sacrifice associates us with the sacrifice of Christ. It associates us not just with "the suffering servant" of the Old Testament (especially Isa. 52:14–53, 1–10), who according to one view is the whole of the Jewish people, but also with "the supreme high priest" (Heb. 4:14) of the New Testament. And this kind of sacrifice identifies us with the divine act of Thérèse offering herself as a "holocaust," and with Etty as a "balm for all wounds." And it is *divine* because it represents the heavenly gift of the power of love as opposed to the love of power. This is "loving as he loved you," as with Paul, "giving himself up in our place as a fragrant offering and a sacrifice to God." For Paul, this is ultimately to follow Christ.

But who is this "Christ"? As so often, I have little original to offer and shall offer relatively little, but I hope his spirit is suffused throughout this essay. Let us forego here exalted titles like Lord, proclaimed at Pentecost, for more companionable designations like "the suffering servant," someone "gentle and humble in heart" (Matt. 12:29). Two of my favorite words of Scripture are "Jesus wept" (John 11:35). This was upon being informed of the death of Lazarus. "Still sighing," the apostle continues,

"Jesus reached the tomb." But then followed the climactic cry, echoing across the centuries: "Lazarus, come forth!" All the same, the greater miracle for me is in the humanity of this man. And this humanity is enshrined not just in his love of "the little ones" but in the enduring of his own "night" experience. "He was troubled in spirit" (John 13:21). "Now is my soul troubled" (John 12:27). But he could still issue in that incomparable prayer of self-transcendence: "Father, glorify thy name" (12:28). What "holy oblivion"! No wonder he could say, *before the end*, "I am in the world no longer" (John 17:11). And what humanity in that cry of abandonment from the Cross: "Why hast Thou foresaken me?" For me, when Christ is most human, he is somehow most divine. And if *he* was not divine, there is no way we will ever be.

This man is a koan incarnate. He "emptied himself" (Phil. 2:7) "that he might fill all things" (Eph. 4:10). An *apparent* failure, he "conquered the world" (John 17:33). The meek Lamb of the Paschal Mystery archetypically embodies life through death.

Friedrich von Hügel has given us, in a paragraph, the best synopsis of this man that I have ever seen. It is too long to quote here, but permit me to quote from its first sentence and its last:

> For a Person came, and lived and loved, and did and taught, and died and rose again, and lives on by His Power and His Spirit for ever within us and amongst us, so unspeakably rich and yet so simple, so sublime and yet so homely, so divinely above us precisely in being so divinely near, —that His character and teaching require, for an ever fuller yet never complete understanding . . . the simultaneous and successive experiences of the whole human race to the end of time. . . . And in Him, for the first and last time, we find an insight so unique, a Personality so strong and supreme, as to teach us, once for all, the true attitude towards suffering.[5]

This teaching is personalized and prefigured in the Johannine: "He had always loved those who were in the world, but now he showed how perfect his love was" (13:1). This he revealed through love as immolation—divine sacrifice.

He spoke of himself as "the Way" (John 14:6), the original name of the Christian community (Acts 9:2). I sometimes muse that it might have been better had we retained that name, for various reasons, including that it makes explicit that it is a way until the end. Not for nothing could that theologian despite himself, James Joyce, in his *A Portrait of the Artist as a Young Man*, issue his cautionary about "the house where young men are called by their Christian names a little too soon." His was a portrait of more than one house of Christendom.

The gospel, by the same token, is intended as more than one portrait of Christ. Christ is "the way," and his sacrifice is not over, not until human suffering is over, for he is in the midst of it. Christ is there, mysteriously living our lives throughout human history, if we would let him. This recapitulation of our lives is resonated in the rhythms of the liturgy. But by the same token, we can be called to live and die his life. This kind of communion is more accessible than we imagine. I think of a passage of Karl Rahner:

> There must be a surrender of the whole man from his uncontrollable and impenetrable existence to the incomprehensible God. Whenever a man dies in this way, believing in confidence, detached from all that is particular and concrete, and with free trust that he will obtain everything, whenever a man apparently experiences a falling down into emptiness, into the fathomless abyss, then he does something that could not have been achieved except by the grace of Christ which celebrates its victory in this very abyss of emptiness. There, man does not die the death of Adam . . . but he dies the death of Christ.[6]

"No one can die for us," we are told. Yes and no. One cannot only die for us but "through" us, "with" us, and "in" us, to vary the liturgical formula. *Who Dies?*, in this light, if the author might appropriate the title of Stephen Levine? Truly, *who* dies?

Sacrifice associates, and we are ultimately in the crucible ourselves, for the sacrifice is *both* unique *and* perpetual. Paul speaks: "Now I rejoice in my sufferings for your sake, and in my flesh I complete what is lacking in Christ's afflictions" (Col. 1:24). Again, echoing the Old Testament: "For your sake we are being massacred daily and reckoned as sheep for the slaughter (Rom. 8:36). Finally, at the Last Supper, Christ took the bread, *broke it*, identified himself with it, and said "Do this in remembrance of me."

This leads us at last to the Paschal Mystery. The Paschal Mystery expresses the essence of the faith. It is celebrated in the liturgy and is the center of evangelical faith over all the centuries. Still, I was surprised to sense the relative paucity or terseness of theological studies on the subject. There are voluminous studies of the Passion and wrangling over particulars of the Resurrection, but if I am not mistaken, comparatively few elucidating the mysterious life through death of the Paschal Mystery. If so, this may be because it is not something to be studied but something to be experienced. There is simply nothing to be said about it. It is a koan, but for once, a koan that is perfectly clear. Its idiom is not linguistic, but carnal, in "the Word made flesh."

Purgatory on Earth:
St. Catherine of Genoa and Caryll Houselander

Confronted with that last ominous journey to Jerusalem, Thomas, in an outburst of windy enthusiasm, exclaimed: "Let us also go, and die with him (John 11:16). This enthusiasm, upon later discovery, Thomas and the scattered apostles would live to repent. Let us again take courage from a woman.

She is St. Catherine of Genoa. Here we might disclose the full title of von Hügel's classic, *The Mystical Element of Religion as Studied in Saint Catherine of Genoa and Her Friends*. Let us pause with her for awhile, and perhaps we too shall become her friends. St. Catherine can be seen as standing somewhere between St. Thérèse and Etty Hillesum. She was a canonized saint, but she was not cloistered, living in self-giving service in the world. She was never a member of a religious community, and she was even a married woman. Though she never directly wrote anything, her thoughts were faithfully recorded and edited by her disciples. Her works include a classic treatise on purgatory which, as I hope we shall see, along with her life, certainly entitle her to a place in "purgatory on earth."

Caterina Fieschi Adorno (1447–1510) was a child of the Italian Renaissance. But she belongs to no age, or virtually any. She is among the most universal of mystics, no doubt a reason von Hügel elected her as the model of his masterpiece. Her influence was incalculable. She has been seen as *the* person who began the reform of the then dissolute Italian church. Though no theologian in the formal sense, it has been advanced that she had an impact upon St. John of the Cross, and "astonishing analogies" have been drawn between their works.[7] Her conception of purgatory was incorporated by John Henry Newman in what was perhaps his most magnificent poem, "The Dream of Gerontius," set to music by Edward Elgar. She has long enjoyed a Protestant following, and analogies have been discerned between her perfectionism and that of John Wesley. There are even Eastern analogies, with kinship between her conception of self and that of the Buddhist doctrine of no self (*anatta*). Still, her spirituality is essentially traditional, but it exemplifies the finest values of tradition.

For all this, her external life appears relatively uneventful. St. Catherine was of a noble Genovese family. At thirteen her desire to enter the convent was frustrated by her parents, and at sixteen this elegant beauty was married away by them to a man as dissolute as she was devout. Driven to despair, a despair apparently compounded by her own lapsing into "worldly vanities" that did not honor her true self, in 1473, while in a church, she was suddenly overwhelmed by an extraordinary experience of the immense love of God. After this she never looked back.

Catherine had been overwhelmed by the immensity of a gratuitous love, and she herself became in turn one of history's most ardent devotees of the doctrine of pure love. Pure love is love for love's (i.e., God's) sake. Pure love is love purified of self-interest, including the dread of hell. It is Bernard's "I love because I love," love as an end in itself. And so potent was this pure love that it even converted her husband, who consented eventually to living as brother and sister, himself ending a Tertiary Franciscan. Catherine preferred God alone, but her interior voice prompted her to the service of humankind, proclaiming "Whoever would love me, loves all that I have loved." For the second half of her life she volunteered for service in a Genovese hospital, heroically ministering to the sick and destitute, including ministering during a time of devastating plague. Her body still keeps vigil beside the hospital today.

St. Catherine's essay on purgatory is her most original work. Her "purgatorial catharsis"[8] joins heaven and earth. Von Hügel speaks of Catherine's "insistence upon an unbroken spiritual life, in spite of, and right through physical death."[9] In other words, purgation or purification is a process, and a process that takes place on a continuum, in this life or in the next—or even right through both of them. Moreover, this is a process that the soul itself longs for, lest it presume to be admitted imperfectly before the Perfect One; lest, to enlist the parable, the bride present herself at the wedding banquet without proper nuptial attire. Newman sums up her sense of purgatory in the instructions of the angels to the soul of Gerontius:

And these two pains, so counter and so keen—
The longing for Him, when thou seest Him not;
The shame of self at thought of seeing Him—
Will be thy veriest, sharpest purgatory.[10]

Accordingly, purgatory itself represents simultaneous joy-in-suffering, and it is "awesome." Yet one might even say that it is reasonable, since it responds to something intrinsic to the sense of order of the soul. Ladislaus Boros, of whom we have spoken in Chapter 2,[11] suggests that purgatory may be the purifying gaze of Christ at the instant of our "final decision." In all events, Catherine has put mystical purgation and purgatory on a common plane, and those who do not pass through it in the former will be satisfied with it in the latter. Her doctrine does not violate the divine mercy but embodies it.

Catherine's health broke utterly in the last decade of her life. Like Thérèse's offering herself as a "holocaust" and Etty's as a "balm," Catherine made a gift of herself to God such that "nothing will be seen of my own proper self" and that "your pure love . . . will annihilate me."[12] The expression of sacrifice might outdo even these saving heroines.

And Catherine's prayer may have been answered. Her annihilation seemed total. "Our God is a consuming fire," warned the author of Hebrews (12:29), and she was consumed. Her kind of love she spoke of as "a loving fire" (*il fuoco amoroso*), and she was immolated in it. Physically, her health failed, and though an abundance of attending physicians testified that hers was a supernatural malady, there is also evidence of cancer, for which her figure of "fire" is not at all inappropriate. Psychologically, in the eyes of the world, she was at times beside herself, and her disciples describe her prayers as "sighs, cries, and inner fire." Her memory was reduced to things divine. At times she felt alien to things spiritual as well as human, even if at one point she stretched out her arms as if nailed to the Cross, her appearance a reflection of an inner crucifixion. Two weeks before the end, her disciples reported that Catherine saw "herself without soul and without body, as she always wished to be, with her spirit completely in God . . . as if she no longer existed."[13] And in the last several days, the fire in which she was being consumed was such that "she asked those present to open the window to see whether the world was on fire."[14] Catherine had become holocaust, incense, a fragrant offering and a sacrifice to God." Her most famous saying was: "My 'Me' is God."[15] And that was what was left of her at the end.

For a final and more contemporary model, let us reflect in passing upon Caryll Houselander (1901–54). An Englishwoman, author, and fellow-sufferer, her life, about which she was not given to complain, was one long heartbreak. Hers was a broken home—effectively orphaned at nine—a broken and impossible romance with Sydney Reilly, the English superspy, religious alienation, and cancer but eventually reconciliation, acceptance, and peace.

I shall content myself to quote from her *The Risen Christ*, in a chapter entitled "The Prayer of the Body," written when her own body was wracked with cancer:

> When we are young, in the full vigour of love, the prayer of the body is a thing of delight. . . . our sense of well-being is something like a shout of praise to God, our five senses like five angels bringing us the messages of his love with touches and tongues of fire. . . .
>
> Sooner or later, our prayer of the body becomes . . . the falling away of self . . . sickness, old age, death; these must come, and when they come it seems that our service is ended. . . .
>
> Everything falls away from us, even memories—even the weariness of self. This is the breaking of the bread, the supreme moment in the prayer of the body, the end of the liturgy of our mortal lives, when we are broken for and in the communion of Christ's love to the whole world.

But it is not the end of the prayer of the body. To that there is no end. Our dust pays homage to God, until the endless morning of resurrection wakens our body, glorified.[16]

"Our dust pays homage to God." This sentence is enough to retire one's pen. But what are we to be *besides* the "dust"? What comes *after* "the sacrifice"? It is to such questions that we turn as we begin to say goodnight.

Concluding Reflections: Glory

It is ultimately for each to write his or her own conclusions, with his or her own life. Yet there is a meditative text to which we are all apt to resonate, a text attributed to St. Francis, though it would seem to encapsulate human experience from Socrates to humanistic psychology, and it is to that meditation that we shall turn for a concluding recollection. Query or prayer, it is: "Who are You, O God, and who am I?" Its second part may be as inscrutable as the first. Our last paradox is this: God is revealed, but *we* are hidden. We are hidden at least since our faulted first parents "hid among the trees of the garden." And we are hidden mostly from ourselves.

All too easy would it be to conclude from this that God and humankind are as far apart as heaven and earth, but "heaven *and* earth are full of" God's "glory." This glory is the primal Sanctus, and it has tremulous personal application: "I have given them the glory that you gave to me" (John 17: 22). This can be intoxicating talk, and in some traditions, e.g., Buddhism, such matters are deemed so impenetrable that a reverent silence is likely to be observed on questions of "God-talk"—essentially the idiom of theodicy. In the West, generally, "silence is golden" but insufficient. With us, there is a tradition of a word that rises out of the silence. Nowhere have I seen this more majestically expressed than in the Book of Wisdom (18:14–15):

When peaceful silence lay over all,
and night had run the half of her swift course,
down from the heavens, from the royal throne,
leapt your all-powerful Word.

Let us begin where we are, applying the word to ourselves in our hiddenness. Since "the Word was made
flesh"—a cornerstone of the faith—so close are God and
humankind that to illuminate the one may be to illuminate the other. This we are likely to know, whether as an
article of faith or a fact of experience: Separated from
God, we do not make "sense." Sooner or later, all is vain
and "absurd." Very likely, all our sanguinary revolutions
to end absurdity, whether of Left or Right, are also in
vain. These revolutions will be vain especially if they are
not respecters of the inalienable "personal."

Person itself is a vast mystery. God is personal but
also transpersonal (Love, Light, Life). In some root sense,
a *persona* is more than a mask. It is that "through" which
something "sounds" (*per-sonare*), perhaps whispers of
that "all-powerful Word," emergent from the silence. In
this view, we ourselves as persons share the mysterious
intimacy of trinitarian life, from which we originate and
to which we are destined. The movement of creation, accordingly, is from that *within* God to that *without*, that is,
from a seminal, transcendent existence to what we know
as concrete, individuated existence, actualized in time.
That at least was the judgement of St. Augustine, especially as elucidated by sympathetic and creative spirits
like Daniel Walsh and his master student, Thomas Merton.[17] Though his theology may have been different, no
wonder the psalmist could be struck with awe: "I will
praise thee; for I am fearfully *and* wonderfully made"
(AV 139:14).

Our "hiddenness" is usually discussed in terms of the
problem of self-knowledge, which the foregoing comments
on the transcendent origins of personality might help illuminate. As a Karl Rahner would say: *We* are "the ques-

tion."[18] We can shoot the moon, but twenty-five centuries after Socrates enunciated his great imperative, "Know thyself," we still do not know what it means to be human. *We* may be the ultimate koan, a fusion, if not confusion, of flesh and spirit. Were we only the one or the other, we could be as concrete as a tree or as abstract as an angel, both quite definite, and accordingly delivered of identity problems. But we are not. Self-knowledge without God-knowledge is likely to lead to self-delusion and despair. Small wonder Sigmund Freud held that self-knowledge is our core repression, and he may have been more theologian than he knew.

We may have been trying too hard. Self-revelation may be inseparable from divine revelation, and that most accessible revelation, the Book of Genesis, informs us that we are images of God. But we may not know what this means until the end. Dame Julian of Norwich, a miracle of the English Middle Ages, illuminates this in chapter 46 of her revelations, or *Showings*:

> And when we know and see, truly and clearly, what our self is, then we shall truly and clearly see and know our Lord God in the fullness of joy. . . . But we may never know ourselves until the last moment.[19]

Paul says much the same. "You have died," he writes, in one of the most riveting lines of Scripture, "and now the life you have is hidden with Christ in God. But when Christ is revealed—and he is your life—you too will be revealed in all your glory with him" (Col. 3:3–4). Again, it is "your glory," and Paul seems to intimate that self-revelation is inseparable from a mysterious process of self-transcendence and glorification. To return once more to that text already cited twice: "And we, with our unveiled faces reflecting like mirrors the brightness of the Lord, all grow brighter and brighter as we are turned into the image that we reflect." "Brighter and brighter," closer and closer, and it is as though in death we walk through the mirror.

Dante begins the last canto of his *Commedia*, the canto that issued in his resplendent Beatific Vision, considered by some as the highest point that literature has ever reached, with a prayer to the Madonna that commences: "Virgin Mother, daughter of thy son." This alludes to the circularity of spiritual birthing. We are children of God, but *we* are pregnant with God, too. This need be no more than the other side of the divine "indwelling." The human is a capacity for God, and we are to bring God forth.

The ancient Christian analogy for death is birth. Both death and birth are accompanied by trauma, but death experiences are usually gentle, certainly gentler than birth experiences. The idea of death as birth seems to originate with Paul. This is advanced in one of his most compelling passages and one with universal resonances:

> From the beginning to now the entire creation, as we know, has been groaning in one great act of giving birth; . . . we too groan inwardly as we wait for our bodies to be set free (Rom. 8:22–23).

But *what* is to be born? For this we might turn to Meister Eckhart, who speaks in his sermons of the birth of God in the soul. And this is a nocturnal birth. His key text, as it happens, is that already cited:

> When peaceful silence lay over all,
> and night had run the half of her swift course,
> down from the heavens, from the royal throne,
> leapt your all-powerful Word.

This text, as it also happens, is from the Christmas liturgy.

But for Eckhart, God has not just engendered "one son," but many children.[20] The true son or daughter, according to Eckhart, is "the spiritual man," "the spiritual woman." Life is a unity, and there is a continuity of birthing. As Paul says, "*one* great act of giving birth." And

it is an ever-enlarging circle, that symbol without beginning or end. Mount Tabor is here and now, and as at the
Transfiguration, that voice from "a bright cloud" still
echoes its enchanting refrain: "This is my beloved son"—
"this is my beloved daughter"—"with whom I am well
pleased" (Matt. 17:5). And we can still respond with the
Madonna-to-be: "Be it done to me according to thy word."

But there is no birth without love. We are loved into
existence. By God and by our parents. And we exist by
love. Not Descartes's "I think, therefore I am," but John
the Divine's, as I understand it, "I love, therefore I am"
(I, 3:14–15). The dynamic is correlative: I am loved, therefore I am. Life as a function of love is not so much faith as
it is a fact of experience. Life is unendurable without love.
The circle of love is the same as the circle of birthing. We
are loved into existence, and if only we are open to it, we
are loved out of this existence by a love more magnetic
than mere flesh can endure. And our last love song might
be the refrain of St. John of the Cross in what seems the
climax to the *Living Flame of Love*: "Perfect me now if it
be thy will."

Love seeks union, and love loves to declare this
union. Love cries out for its rite of celebration: Marriage.
Marriage, our great symbol, celebrates the passage from
longing to belonging. Marriage is now itself a problem,
judged by cynics as readied for its own last rites. Or is it,
to the contrary, the *only* relationship with a future? There
may not be "giving and taking in marriage" in heaven, for
all will be already married!

Our final metaphor is not unfitting. It has been seen
as the central and unifying theme of divine revelation.
Marriage symbols abound. The very first words ascribed
to man are in fact a marriage formula: "This at last is
bone of my bones and flesh of my flesh (Gen. 2:23). In, as
it were, the centerpiece, Christ is greeted as the "Bridegroom" (John 3:29). And the climax is "the wedding feast
of the Lamb" (Rev. 19:9).

It is this union with the Lamb, our great symbol of
the sacrifice, that is our pledge of life without end. "There

will be no more death." "And there will be no night there."
For the "holy city" is lit by the immolation of the Lamb
and the burnt men and women of God, a fire that, like the
Burning Bush, does not consume. Whatever we may look
like, no matter how tattered this wedding garment, we
are the "bride." And a text for mystical union of St. John
of the Cross is the song addressed to the bride (Song of
Songs 2:10–11):

> Arise, my love, my fair one, and come away;
> for lo, the winter is past, the rain is over
>   and gone . . .
> The flowers appear on the earth, the time of
>   singing has come;
> and the voice of the turtledove is heard in our
>   land.

Wedded means "oned." With this, the two parts of
our concluding query and prayer seem dissolved into one.
And at the end there *is* more than dust, even "the dust of
death." There is the same thing there was at the beginning, a mysterious love greater than death. This is the
love that "urges" us on. So that somehow, at the end, in
the immortal and immortalizing words of St. Augustine,
there is only "One Christ, loving himself."

Afterword

To express hope as by a star, the eagerness of a soul by a radiant sunset.

—Vincent Van Gogh to his brother Theo (1888)

Glory is incandescent and ascentional, and we have tried to show that "the dying of the light" can be a dawning; requiem, a rainbow.

Our recourse to a nocturnal theology was by no means to rejoice in some starless night, but to suggest that one cannot see the stars save by night. Nocturnal theology is a means to an end, and night herself is handmaiden of the light.

In some sense this has been an essay on light and on love. Love is itself illuminative, and *if* in our climactic chapter we have taken it to its consummation ("Greater love than this hath no one"—John 15:13), let us now attempt to follow the light to its source. Let us honor our vocation to the light, to enlightenment, and not least to "the light of the world (John 8:12)."

Obscure it may sometimes be, but this essay was inspired by the light, and it aspires to the true light. It proceeded from the fear of the child, and by no means just the child, of "the dark at the top of the stairs." The essential

101

idea was inspired by a gallant teenager, Burlena Turner, who grew afraid of sleep, "Death of each day's life," and sought recourse in the artificial light of television. She went on to become a child of the light. Some years later this essay was conceived as a book while on sabbatical at Berkeley. I believe that it was conceived there in the Rose Garden, a reflection upon the light of the sunset, itself a bittersweet metaphor for the tragic spectre of the AIDS crisis across the bay in the city named after St. Francis. From this it gained urgency, but the bell would have to toll for all, and it would be a book about the human condition. The author had offered seminars in the mystical and spiritual classics for almost twenty years, but after this experience at Berkeley he especially deepened himself in the mystical theology of St. John of the Cross. Here was light *and* love, as suggested in the very title, *Sayings of Light and Love,* and concretized in its compelling, "In the evening of life you will be examined in love."[21] The mystical theology of John was an extraordinary ingathering of light and darkness, kindred to what Renaissance art called chiaroscuro ("clear/dark"), of which Caravaggio and Rembrandt were such masters. Light rises from and glows in the darkness—and miraculously, Christ is breaking bread with the pilgrims of Emmaus. A conceptual and, I hope, creative fusion of the light of Burlena, the Rose Garden at Berkeley, and the Mystical Doctor was more or less spontaneous and natural. Light is one, or would be one, if we would let it.

Light is a great miracle, and it can be seen as God's first gift (Gen. 1:3), the primal sacrament. The gift is likely to be most cherished when, it would seem, least in supply. As with winter light, if you will. And so the author, having enjoyed his three score years, finds himself increasingly fascinated with the mystery of light. This fascination would seem anticipated by and endemic to naturally "benighted" primitive peoples, with their ubiquitous sacred hearths and sun gods.

The dawn of the Age of Faith inspired a whole metaphysics of light. A synthesis of grace and nature, it was blended, above all, of the light theology centered in the prologue of the gospel of St. John the Divine, and of various currents of natural theology from Neoplatonism. A consequence was that that age did not suffer our separation of spiritual and natural light. Light was the first principle of creation and of creativity, that which infused all of being, the reconciler of all things. There was a whole aesthetic of light. This may be a reason that the icons of that age could be infused with such an uncanny spiritual power, the effect of those rose windows so endearing, the evening's play of light and shadow on Gothic church-walls so meditative, the chanting of the *Lux aeterna* of the Requiem so penetrating, and the *Showings* of a Julian, one of a host of luminaries, so indelible. The world was more visual and more visionary.

Dante is generally considered the consummation of this worldview. The metaphysics of light would be lost. Mother nature would be devitalized and dissected, light sundered and secularized by the critical spirit of the early Enlightenment, and, if I am not mistaken, spiritual light self-destructed in the extravagant and contrived luminosity of the baroque. The psalmist had cautioned: "In *thy* light do we see light" (35:10).

We are in peril of being spiritually blinded in a superfluity of artificial light. A world of cultivated, even boxed and packaged light, conditions us to be blind and "unironic" to the light that is residual in darkness and the darkness that is residual in our own light. We do not see the stars save by night, and we are unlikely to see them save removed from the cultivated light of the city. We cannot all reside in nature, but she is still our oldest resident teacher or, to be more precise, illustrator. And she is rich enough to provide reminders of the miracle of light in the wordless magnificat of the late October leaves, simultaneously requiem and rainbow. Their very passage is praise.

Death is ultimately too deep for tragedy, and let us return at last to the *Commedia* of Dante, the great poet of the light. If Dante takes us to hell and back, the *Paradiso* is suffused with light. His saints can be *hidden* in the light. All three parts of the *Commedia* end with the word "stars" (*stelle*), symbol of his hope. At first blinded by spiritual light, Dante climaxes in the Beatific Vision. Words fail, and Dante turns to the trinitarian figure of threefold spheres of light, of "rainbow from rainbow," weaving a celestial "smile." Dante said: "I gazed." Who would not, for words are not equal to such wonderment?

Dante gazed, and so should we. Done is our own nocturnal passage, illumined by the same Easter fire, and it is as dawn. May the wounded pilgrim be healed and any "midnight phantoms" vanquished by the ancient hymn to the victory of dawn, the *Aurora,* with which we prefaced our descent into the night. And may the turning to the light in dread, which began this essay, be a turning to the light in adoration, where it would end.

At the beginning, God said, "Let there be light." There was, and God "saw that it was good." God gazed. This vision was "the simple enjoyment of the truth," and, in the words of the Angelic Doctor, it was prayer. It was the first prayer. If we care, it is ours to end as on that first day of creation, with the primal prayer in the primal, and eternal, light.

NOTES

Preface

1. (New York: The Free Press, 1973), 285.

Chapter 1

1. Ed. Sally Fitzgerald (New York: Vintage, 1980), 100.

2. (Minneapolis: Augsburg, 1979). For a discussion, one can see the author's "Mystical and Evangelical Theology in Martin Luther and St. John of the Cross," *Journal of Ecumenical Studies*, XXVIII (Fall, 1991), 555–66.

3. "The Need to Know and the Fear of Knowing," *The Journal of General Psychology*, LXVII (1963), 118.

4. Louis Bouyer, *The Spirituality of the New Testament and the Fathers, A History of Christian Spirituality* (3 vols.; New York: Crossroads, 1963–68), I, 418.

5. (New York: Bantam, 1961), 201–2.

6. Thomas Merton wrote at the beginning of *New Seeds of Contemplation* (New York: New Directions; 1962), 2, that "To enter into the realm of contemplation one must in a certain sense die." Among others, Abraham Maslow, *Religions, Values and Peak-Experiences* (New York: Viking, 1970), 76, writes: "Ecstasy is somehow close to death experience . . . sweet death, that is;" Beatrice Bruteau, *The Psychic Grid* (Wheaton, Ill.: Theosophical Publishing House, 1979), 141, speaks of the death

of the ego, noting the implicit similitude between mystical experience and death; Ignace Lepp, *Death and Its Mysteries*, trans. Bernard Murchand (New York: Macmillan, 1968), 9, has a paragraph on the matter. The idea runs through some of the haunting work of John S. Dunne, especially with his very fertile and key *motif* of "passing over;" See especially *The House of Wisdom* (San Francisco: Harper and Row, 1985), chapter 4: "There Are Signs," pp. 80–93.

7. For a statement on Paul and the mysteries, see A. Wikenhauser, *Pauline Mysticism* (Freiburg: Herder, 1960), 183–89. Also see Albert Schweitzer, *The Mysticism of Paul the Apostle* (1931; New York: Crossroads, 1968), 126–27, who stresses the originality of Paul in advancing that the dying and rising are continuous, not just once.

8. Ida Fredericke Görres, *The Hidden Face: A Study of St. Thérèse of Lisieux*, trans. Richard and Clara Winston (New York: Pantheon, 1959), 270.

9. *The Confessions of St. Augustine*, trans. Rex Warner (New York: Mentor, 1963), 200–202.

10. "St. Francis of Assisi: Christian Mysticism at the Crossroads," ed. Stephen Katz, *Mysticism and Religious Traditions* (London: Oxford University Press, 1983), 164.

11. *First and Second Life of St. Francis*, in *St. Francis of Assisi: Omnibus of Sources*, ed. Marion A. Habig (Chicago: Franciscan Herald Press, 1983), 309.

12. For quotes on a *Clockwork Orange,* see the caveat and last book of R. C. Zaehner, *Our Savage God: The Perverse Use of Eastern Thought* (New York: Sheed and Ward, 1969), 268. For Eliade, *The Two and the One* (original title *Mephistopheles and the Androgyne*), trans. J. M. Cohen (New York: Harper Torchbooks, 1969), 100. On the other hand, we might add that Christ himself could speak of his "glory" as inclusive of both death and resurrection (John 12:23), a thought from James Somerville, "The Mystical Sense of the Gospel, VIII," *The Roll of the Schola Contemplationis* (June, 1993).

13. On Cusa, see Jasper Hoskins, *Nicholas of Cusa's Dialectical Mysticism, Text, Translation and Interpretation of* De Visione dei (Minneapolis: A. J. Banning, 1985), and Hoskins, *On Learned Ignorance, Translation and Appraisal of* De docta

ignorancia (Minneapolis: A. J. Banning, 1981). There is some comment, we might add, on affinities between the thought of Cusa and some Eastern modalities. Fascinatingly, Morimichi Watanabe, himself dean of Cusanists, informs me that Cusa has influenced the great Kyoto school of philosophy in Japan. International Medieval Colloquium, Western Michigan University, 11 June, 1993.

14. *Love and Learning* (New York: Harvest Books, 1985), 10. For the author's exploration, see "Merton, the Coincidence of Opposites and the Archaeology of Catholicity," *Cistercian Studies Quarterly*, XXVI (1991), 257–70.

15. *The Human Journey. Thomas Merton: Symbol of a Century* (Garden City, N.Y.: Image-Doubleday, 1984), 97.

16. For the author's theological exploration of the face, see "Theological Table-Talk: The Face as Theology," *Theology Today*, XLI (October, 1984), 314–20.

17. *The Life of Teresa of Jesus*, trans. E. Allison Peers (Garden City, N.Y.: Image-Doubleday, 1960), 274–75. For the author's discussion of the literature, "The Passion of St. Teresa," *The Month*, CCXLIV (July, 1982), 242–45.

18. *Mysticism Sacred and Profane* (London: Oxford University Press, 1961), 151.

19. According to witnesses of her death and even a medical examination of her heart. See Gabriel de Ste. Marie Madeleine, "L'École Thérésienne et les blessures d'amour mystique," *Études Carmelitaines* (1936), especially, 223–27, 233–35.

20. See especially Kenneth Ring, *Life at Death: A Scientific Investigation of Near-Death Experience* (New York: Quill, 1982).

21. Translations of the poetry of John of the Cross are the author's own. For the original, see S. Juan de la Cruz, "Cantico Espiritual," *Obras Completas* (Burgos: Editorial de Monte Carmelo, 1990), 18.

22. (Berkeley: University of California Press, 1969), 111.

23. *Sermo CXXX. Patrologiae cursus completus, Series latina* ed. J. P. Migne (221 vols., Paris: 1878–90), 39: 1987.

24. This is not the time and place to mine the rich paradoxes of the wound of love and the wounded healer, but I would venture a few observations. The principle that death cures death, if you will, may be the highest moral realization of the archaic medical philosophy of homeopathy, "like cures like." Homeopathic healing is premised upon a certain natural sympathy between ailment and antidote. If its language (including heteropathic healing, for the two can mix) is no older than several centuries, elements of it can be found in the Father of Medicine, Hippocrates, and it has universal resonances. We know it from vaccination, and it is still broadly applied in Native American, Latin American, and Asian Cultures.

Our interest in homeopathy is, of course, in spiritual healing. One of the greatest statements of it in our literature is none other than *The Praise of Folly* of Erasmus of Rotterdam. Folly responds to and would disarm the epidemic of madness of the Renaissance with the divine "madness" of laughter. The logic of homeopathy is implicit in a great spiritual master like John of the Cross. For example, his *The Living Flame of Love,* with its extraordinary "cautery of love," is a magnificent and, I suspect, largely unexplored treasure of homeopathic healing. To quote it again: "the more it wounds, the more it heals" (2:7). The mysterious logic of homeopathy represents not an invasion of magical thinking, of course, but the inclusion of a preternatural wisdom. It bespeaks the hunger for wholeness of even mute creation. Did not Paul himself write of "the entire creation as . . . groaning in one great act of giving birth" (Rom. 8:22)? To some of this we shall recur.

25. Broch, who scores "the flight into beauty," says of his great but spiritually exhausted Roman poet, Virgil: "In his own life, in his own work, he had experienced the seduction of un-art, the seduction of all substitution which puts the thing created in the place of that which creates, the game in place of communion, the fixed thing in the place of the living, ever-vital principle, beauty in the place of truth . . . adulterating death with beauty and beauty with death . . . one who desires to create love through beauty, because he confuses what is created with that which creates." Trans. Jean Starr Untermeyer (Gloucester, Mass.: Peter Smith, 1976) 142, 150. Though Broch is unfortunately not well-known, George Steiner has rated him the greatest European novelist since James Joyce.

26. *Immortality of the Soul or Resurrection of the Body?* (London: Epsworth, 1958), 22. At a conference at Oxford some years ago, it was also advanced that atheists die more contentedly than Christians. See Tony Smith, "Christianity and the Dying," *British Medical Journal* 291 (1985), 1223. For Nietzsche, fear of death was "a European sickness," i.e., a Christian sickness, according to Karl Jaspers, *Nietzsche*, trans. Charles Wallraff and Frederick Schmitz (Tuscon: University of Arizona Press, 1965), 323. Helmut Thielicke responded in effect that Nietzsche had his own problems: "Hubris and nihilism, selfdivinization and insanity are here in frightful proximity to one another." *Death and Life*, trans. Edward Schroder (Philadelphia: Fortress, 1970), 27. It should go without saying that *if* there is inordinate fear of death among Christians, the intent of the author is to understand it—and address it. And for the present record, it should be said that the evidence is that countless saints belie the assumption here. John of the Cross, for example, died with great serenity despite the most trying circumstances. Thomas More was positively jocular at the scaffold. To be sure, this is matter for a separate study.

27. For example, *Death and Eastern Thought*, ed. Frederick H. Holck (Nashville: Abingdon, 1974), 19, 131, 161.

28. "The Recurrence," in *Collected Poems* (New York: Grove, 1953), 74.

29. Holck, 10. For some general support on our comparative sense, see the differences between myth and history in Mircea Eliade, *Myth and Reality*, trans. Willard Trask (New York: Harper and Row, 1963). On time, see Oscar Cullman, *Christ and Time*, trans. Floyd V. Filson (1948; Philadelphia: Westminster, 1950); *Cultures and Time*, intro. Paul Ricoeur (Paris: UNESCO Press, 1976); and the insightful essay of Abraham Joshua Heschel, *The Sabbath* (1951; New York: Farrar, Strauss and Giroux, 1984). For a modern variant see David Gross, "Space, Time and Modern Culture," *Telos* L (Winter 1981–82), 59–78.

When all is said and done, the "Indian difference" could hardly be expressed as well by ethnology as it was by a Taos Native American:

God put the Indians on the earth, and after that the white people. But they were separated by something. By time. Indians have no time. They have never had no time. Now the white people, God He told them to change. And so changing began when the white people came in the world. But he told the Indians to stay themselves; not to change. He never put change in the Indians. The white people have to change, that is their way. So they try to change everything. . . . They want to change people and nations and will not let them be.

Quoted in Mabel Dodge Luhan, *Edge of Taos Desert: An Escape to Reality* (1937; Albuquerque: University of New Mexico Press, 1987), 199, 280.

30. (Garden City, N.Y.: Anchor-Doubleday, 1982). But see also Becker, *The Denial of Death*, 12, who is critical here of Hinduism and Buddhism as performing "the ingenious trick of pretending not to want to be reborn," presumably a variation on *denial*. We might also note that though Buddhists have a doctrine of reincarnation, they do not have a doctrine of a *soul* to be reincarnated. What is perpetuated are ever-changing "aggregates" or energies of the person. It is a perpetuation of inpermanence. Also see Edward Conze, *Buddhist Wisdom Books* (New York: Harper and Row, 1958), 89ff.

31. Ignace Lepp, *Death and Its Mysteries*, trans. Bernard Murchand (New York: Macmillan, 1968), 61. Also supportive and conceived with a comparative sense is Richard Wolff, *The Last Enemy* (Washington, D.C.: Canon Press, 1974).

32. Ed. W. Y. Evans-Wentz (London: Oxford University Press, 1927).

33. (San Francisco: HarperCollins, 1992). It goes without saying that broad cultural configurations compare as well as contrast, and there is Eastern support for our association of mysticism and death. As the Dalai Lama recently put it: "One of the aims of Tantra is to enable the practitioner to 'experience' death, for it is then that the most powerful spiritual realizations can come about." *Freedom in Exile: The Autobiography of Dalai Lama* (New York: HarperCollins, 1990), 210. And the ecumenical Keiji Nishitani reveals the Zen saying, "Beneath the Great Death, the Great Enlightenment," in *Religion and Nothingness*, trans. Jan van Bragt (Berkeley: University of California Press, 1982), 21. He also corroborates my basic construction (p. 212): "Christianity broke down the cyclical character of mythical time and imparted historicity to time."

34. For particulars and context, see the author's *Masks of Satan: The Demonic in History* (1983; Westminster, Md.: Christian Classics, 1989), 170.

35. *The Book of Job* (New York: Harper Perennial, 1992), 79, 84.

36. For a token of his range, one can consult the author's "Satori in St. John of the Cross," *Bulletin of Monastic Interreligious Dialogue*, 47, (May, 1993), 13–18, and the author's essay on John and Luther, cf. note 2 above.

37. "Cantico Espiritual," *Obras*, 18.

Chapter 2

1. Quoted in his *Poetry and Contemplation in St. John of the Cross* (Athens: Ohio University Press, 1988), 111.

2. *St. Francis of Assisi: Omnibus of Sources*, 1382–83.

3. J. F. Powers, *Wheat That Springeth Green* (New York: Alfred A. Knopf, 1988), 211.

4. One can again refer to R. C. Zaehner, *The Savage God*.

5. Ed. Clifton Wolters (Baltimore, Md.: Penguin Books, 1961), 43.

6. Both quotes are from the E. Allison Peers translation (Garden City, N.Y.: Image-Doubleday, 1959), 100.

7. *Ascent of Mount Carmel* (I, xiii, 11). Trans. E. Allison Peers (3rd rev. ed.; Garden City, N.Y.: Image-Doubleday, 1958), 156. For a more recent and superb edition, see *The Collected Works of St. John of the Cross*, trans. Kieran Kavanaugh, O.C.D., and Otilio Rodriguez, O.C.D. (rev. ed.; Washington, D.C.: Institute of Carmelite Studies, 1991), 150. With reference to John's dipolarity of *nada* and *todo*, the exemplary study of Daniel Dombroski, *St. John of the Cross: An Appreciation* (Albany: State University of New York Press, 1992), 74–75, develops how "apparent opposites energize the thought of John of the Cross" and roots it in a "dipolar theism." John's dipolarity, we might note, insulated him against any perils of illuminism or Gnostic reduction.

8. "Cantico Espiritual," *Obras*, 20.

9. "Noche Oscura," *Obras* , 22.

10. *Dark Night of the Soul* (I, xii, 3), in Peers, 78–79.

11. *The Cloud*, 100.

12. Ibid., 62.

13. F. C. Gardiner, *The Pilgrimage of Desire: A Study of Theme and Genre in Medieval Literature* (Leiden: Brill, 1971).

14. *The Cloud* , 60, 83.

15. Realisation is kindred to Newman's famous distinction between "real assent" and merely "notional assent" in his *Grammar of Assent*. For elucidation of *ascent* from verbalization through "simplification," as in poetry, to "realisation"—apprehension of reality itself—see the classic of Henri Bremond, *Prayer and Poetry*, trans. Algar Thorald (London: Burns, Oates and Washbourne, 1927), especially 91–92.

16. *The Cloud* , 134.

17. WA 31/1: 249, quoted in Paul Althaus, *Theology of Martin Luther*, trans. Robert C. Schultz (Philadelphia: Fortress, 1966), 30.

18. P. 61.

19. The whole problem of prayer, in historical perspective, with practical application, is to be found in his *Open Mind, Open Heart: The Contemplative Dimension of the Gospel* (Amity, N.Y.: Amity House, 1986). Among the many other works in this vein, I can recommend John Main, *Moment of Christ: The Path of Meditation* (New York: Crossroads, 1984), for whom the great monologic prayer is "Maranatha." For a practical East-West application, one can see the culturally Indianized Henri Le Saux, or Abhishiktananda, *Prayer* (Philadelphia: Westminister, 1973).

20. *Meister Eckhart*, trans. Raymond B. Blakney (New York: Harper Torchbooks, 1941), 242–43.

21. For an economical edition: (New York: Frederick Ungar, 1978), 14.

22. Trans. Gregory Bainbridge, O.S.B. (Montreal: Palm Publishers, 1965).

23. I am quoting from the essay of Boros, "Death: A Theological Reflection," in *The Mystery of Suffering and Death*, ed. Michael J. Taylor, S.J. (New York: Alba, 1973), 144, 148, 149.

24. (2 vols.; London: James Clarke, 1908).

25. Trans. Richard and Clara Winston (New York: Vintage, 1973), 109; for Dorothy Soelle, see *Suffering*, trans. Everett R. Kalin (Philadelphia, Fortress, 1975).

26. John Chapman, *Spiritual Letters* (London: Sheed and Ward, 1935), 101.

27. Figures are from Simone de Beauvoir, *The Second Sex*, trans. H. M. Parshley (New York: Bantam, 1961), 637, and are generally supported by the article, "Stigmatisation," *Dictionnaire de théologie catholique*, XIV, pt. 2, 2617–19.

28. Simone Weil, *Waiting on God*, trans. Emma Craufurd (London: Collins, 1959), 49.

29. *The Autobiography of St. Therese of Lisieux: The Story of a Soul*, trans. John Beevers, (1898; Garden City, N.Y.: Image-Doubleday, 1957), 17ff.

30. *Collected Letters of Saint Therese of Liseaux*, trans. F. J. Sheed (New York: Sheed and Ward, 1949), 7.

31. Görres, *The Hidden Face: The Life of Therese of Lisieux*, 360.

32. *An Interrupted Life: The Diaries of Etty Hillesum*, trans. Arno Pomerans (New York: Pantheon, 1983), 1, 196.

33. Ibid., 73.

34. P. 86.

35. See especially Rosemary Haughton, *The Passionate God* (New York: Paulist, 1981). Also see Ann Ulanov, *Receiving Woman* (Philadelphia: Westminister, 1981).

36. P. 89.

37. P. 132.

38 Respectively, 170, and 172.

39. *The Mystical Element of Religion*, II, 27.

40. "Noche Oscura," *Obras*, 22.

41. *Selections from the Protrektikos*, trans. Thomas Merton (New York: New Directions, 1962), 25.

Chapter 3

1. *The Hour of Our Death*, trans. Helen Weaver (New York: Vintage, 1982); *Western Attitudes toward Death*, trans. Patricia Ranum (Baltimore, Md.: Johns Hopkins University Press, 1974). One might also note Russell Aldwinckle, *Death in the Secular City* (London: George Allen and Unwin, 1972).

2. *Death, Sacrifice and Tragedy* (Lincoln: University of Nebraska Press, 1966), 46. Reaffirmed by John Bowker, *The Meanings of Death* (Cambridge University Press, 1991), 41: "Sacrifice . . . is by far the earliest category through which religions explore the nature and significance of death. It is the theme of life yielding not simply *to* life . . . but life yielding *for* life."

3. *Masks of Satan: The Demonic in History*, 15ff.

4. *Tragic Sense of Life*, trans. J. E. Crawford Flitch (1921; New York: Dover, 1954), 64.

5. *The Mystical Element*, I, 26.

6. *On the Theology of Death* (Freiburg: Herder, 1961), 96, 111.

7. Jean Baruzi, *Saint Jean de la Croix et le problème de L'experiénce mystique* (Paris: Felix Alcan, 1931), 597.

8. See the masterwork of P. Umile Bonzi da Genova, *S. Caterina Fieschi Adorno* (2 vols.; Marietta, 1960–62), I, 146. First volume is his magisterial synthesis, second volume his critical edition.

9. Ibid., II, 90.

10. *Verses on Various Occasions* (London: Longmans, Green and Co., 1903), 360.

11. See note 23.

12. Bonzi da Genova, II, 403.

13. Ibid., II, 451.

14. Ibid., II, 455.

15. Ibid., II, 171.

16. (New York: Sheed and Ward, 1958), 66, 73–74.

17. See Robert Imperato, *Merton and Walsh on the Person* (Brookfield, Wisc.: Liturgical Publication, 1987), which I found helpful.

18. *Foundations of the Christian Faith*, trans. William V. Dych (New York: Seabury Press, 1978), 32.

19. Trans. Edmund Colledge and James Walsh (New York: Paulist Press, 1978), 258.

20. The birth of God in the soul can be culled from *Meister Eckhart*, trans. Raymond Bernard Blakney (New York: Harper Torchbooks, 1957), 95–124.

21. *Obras,* 62.

BIBLIOGRAPHY

Ariès, Philippe. *The Hour of Our Death*. Trans. Helen Weaver. New York: Vintage, 1982.

——. *Western Attitudes toward Death*. Trans. Patricia Ranum. Baltimore: Johns Hopkins Press, 1974.

Ars Moriendi: The Book of the Craft of Dying and Other Early English Tracts Concerning Death. London and New York: Longmans, Green and Company, 1917.

Augustine. *The Confessions*. Trans. Rex Warner. New York: Mentor, 1963.

Beauvoir, Simone de. *A Very Easy Death*. London: Weidenfeld, 1966.

Becker, Ernest. *The Denial of Death*. New York: The Free Press, 1973.

Bonzi da Genova, P. Umile. *S. Caterina Fieschi Adorno*. 2 vols. Turino: Marietti, 1960–62.

Bowker, John. *Problems of Suffering in Religions of the World*. Cambridge: Cambridge University Press, 1990.

——. *The Meanings of Death*. Cambridge: Cambridge University Press, 1991.

Boros, Ladislaus. *The Moment of Truth: Mysterium Mortis*. Trans. Gregory Bainbridge. Montreal: Palm Publishers, 1965.

Chapman, John. *Spiritual Letters*. London: Sheed and Ward, 1935.

The Cloud of Unknowing. Ed. Clifton Childers. Baltimore: Penguin, 1961.

Cullmann, Oscar. *Christ and Time*. Trans. Floyd Filson. Philadelphia: Westminster, 1950.

———. *Immortality of the Soul or Resurrection of the Body?* London: Epsworth, 1958.

Choron, Jacques. *Death and Western Man*. New York: The Macmillan Company, 1962.

Dante, Aligieri, *La divina commedia*. Bologna: Nicola Zanichelli, 1958.

Dickens, E. W. Trueman. *The Crucible of Love: A Study of the Mysticism of St. Teresa of Jesus and St. John of the Cross*. New York: Sheed and Ward, 1963.

Dombroski, Daniel. *St. John of the Cross: An Appreciation*. Albany: State University of New York Press, 1992.

Donne, John. *Devotions*. Ann Arbor: University of Michigan Press, 1975.

Doss, Richard W. *The Last Enemy: A Christian Understanding of Death*. New York: Harper and Row, 1974.

Dostoyevsky, Fyodor. *The Brothers Karamazov*. Trans. Constance Garnett. New York: Modern Library, n.d.

Dunne, John S. *The Way of All the Earth*. New York: Macmillan, 1972.

———. *The House of Wisdom*. San Francisco: Harper and Row, 1985.

Eliade, Mircea. *The Two and the One*. Trans. J. M. Cohen. New York: Harper Torchbooks, 1969.

———. *Myth and Reality*. Trans. Willard Trask. New York: Harper and Row Publishers, 1963.

Foss, Martin. *Death, Sacrifice, and Tragedy*. Lincoln: University of Nebraska Press, 1966.

Frankl, Viktor. *The Doctor and the Soul*. Trans. Richard and Clara Winston. New York: Vintage Books, 1973.

Gardiner, F. C. *The Pilgrimage of Desire: A Study of Theme and Genre in Medieval Literature*. Leiden: Brill, 1971.

Gatch, Milton McC. *Death: Meaning and Mortality in Christian Thought and Contemporary Culture*. New York: Seabury, 1969.

Görres, Ida Fredericke. *The Hidden Face: A Study of St. Therese of Lisieux*. Trans. Richard and Clara Winston. New York: Pantheon Books, 1959.

Groeschel, Benedict J. *Spiritual Passages*. New York: Crossroad, 1984.

Gross, David. "Space, Time and Modern Culture," *Telos* L (Winter 1981–82).

Heschel, Abraham Joshua. *The Sabbath*. New York: Farrar, Strauss and Giroux, 1984.

Head, Joseph, and Cranston, S. L., eds. *Reincarnation: An East-West Anthology*. New York: Julian, 1961.

Hillesum, Etty. *An Interrupted Life: The Diaries of Etty Hillesum 1941–43*. New York: Pantheon, 1983.

———. *Letters from Westerbork*. Trans. Arnold J. Pomerans. New York: Pantheon, 1986.

Houselander, Caryll. *The Risen Christ*. New York: Sheed and Ward, 1958.

Holck, Frederick H. *Death and Eastern Thought*. Nashville: Abingdon, 1974.

Hunsinger, George. *Kierkegaard, Heidegger and the Concept of Death*. Stanford, Calif.: Leland Stanford Junior University, 1969.

John of the Cross. *The Collected Works of St. John of the Cross*. Trans. Kieran Kavanaugh, O.C.D., and Otilio Rodriguez, O.C.D. Washington D.C.: Institute of Carmelite Studies, 1991.

———. S. Juan de la Cruz. *Obras Completas*. Burgos, Spain: Editorial Monte Carmelo, 1990.

Kapleau, Philip, ed. *The Wheel of Death*. New York: Harper Colophon Books, 1971.

Kierkegaard, Søren. *The Gospel of Suffering and the Lilies of the Field*. Trans. D. F. and L. M. Swenson. Minneapolis: Augsburg, 1947.

————. *Purity of Heart*. Trans. Douglas V. Steere. New York: Harper & Row, 1956.

Kramer, Kenneth. *The Sacred Art of Dying: How World Religions Understand Death*. New York: Paulist Press, 1988.

Kübler-Ross, Elizabeth. *AIDS: The Ultimate Challenge*. New York: Macmillan, 1987.

————. *On Death and Dying*. New York: Macmillian, 1969.

Küng, Hans. *Eternal Life*. Trans. Edward Quinn. Garden City, N.Y.: Doubleday, 1984.

Kushner, Harold S. *When Bad Things Happen to Good People*. New York: Schocken, 1981.

Léon-Dufour, Xavier. *Life and Death in the New Testament*. Trans. Terrence Prendergast. San Francisco: Harper & Row, 1986.

Lepp, Igance. *Death and its Mysteries*. Trans. Bernard Murchand. New York: Macmillan, 1968.

Levine, Stephen. *Who Dies?* Garden City, N.Y.: Anchor-Doubleday, 1982.

————. *Healing into Life and Death*. New York: Doubleday, 1987.

Lewis, C. S. (pseud. N. W. Clerk). *A Grief Observed*. New York: Seabury Press, 1963.

Lossky, Vladimir. *The Mystical Theology of the Eastern Church*. Crestwood, N.Y.: St. Vladimir's Seminary Press, 1976.

Luhan, Mabel Dodge. *Edge of Taos Desert: An Escape to Reality*. Albuquerque: University of New Mexico Press, 1987.

Marcel, Gabriel. *Tragic Wisdom and Beyond*. Trans. Stephen Jolin and Peter McCormack. Evanston, Ill.: Northwestern University Press, 1973.

Maslow, Abraham. "The Need to Know and the Fear of Knowing." *Journal of General Psychology*, LXVII (1963).

Meister Eckhart. *Meister Eckhart*. Trans. Raymond B. Blakney. New York: Harper Torchbooks, 1941.

May, Gerald. *The Awakened Heart*. San Francisco: Harper-Collins, 1991.

Merton, Thomas. *Love and Learning*. San Diego: Harcourt, Brace, Jovanovich, 1985.

―――. *New Seeds of Contemplation*. New York: New Directions, 1962.

Momeyer, Richard. *Confronting Death*. Bloomington: Indiana University Press, 1988.

Morel, Georges. *Le sens de l'existence selon Saint Jean de la Croix*. 3 vols. Bruges and Paris: Aubier, 1960–61.

Moody, Raymond. *Life After Death*. New York: Bantam, 1977.

Nasr, Seyyed Hossein. *Knowledge and the Sacred*. New York: Crossroad, 1981.

Neale, Robert E. *The Art of Dying*. New York: Harper and Row, 1971.

Nouwen, Henri. *In Memoriam*. Notre Dame, Ind.: Ave Maria Press, 1988.

―――. *A Letter of Consolation*. New York: Harper and Row, 1982.

Nugent, Christopher. *Masks of Satan: The Demonic in History*. Westminster, Md.: Christian Classics, 1989.

―――. "Suicide: Mystical and Material." *Living Prayer*, Vol. XX/2 (March-April, 1987).

Otto, Rudolph. *The Idea of the Holy*. Trans. John W. Harvey. London: Oxford University Press, 1928.

Pelikan, Jaroslav. *The Shape of Death: Life, Death, and Immortality in the Early Fathers*. New York: Abingdon Press, 1961.

Radin, Paul. *Primitive Religion*. New York: Viking, 1937.

Rahner, Karl. *On the Theology of Death*. Freiburg: Herder, 1961.

Ricoeur, Paul, Intro. *Cultures and Time*. Paris: UNESCO Press, 1976.

Ring, Kenneth. *Life at Death: A Scientific Investigation of Near-Death Experience*. New York: Quill, 1982.

Ruiz, Federico. *Mistico y Maestro: San Juan de la Cruz*. Madrid: Editorial de Espiritualidad, 1986.

Sanford, John. *Soul Journey*. New York: Crossroad, 1991.

Sjögren, Per-Olof. *The Jesus Prayer*. Philadelphia: Fortress, 1975.

Soelle, Dorothy. *Suffering*. Trans. Everett R. Kalin. Philadelphia: Fortress, 1975.

Sogyal, Rinpoche. *The Tibetan Book of Living and Dying*. San Francisco: HarperCollins, 1992.

Somerville, James. "The Mystical Sense of the Gospel, VIII." *The Roll of the Schola Contemplationis*. June, 1993.

St. Francis of Assisi. Writings and Early Biographies. Marion A. Habig, ed. Chicago: Franciscan Herald Press, 1983.

Tavard, George. *Poetry and Contemplation in St. John of the Cross*. Athens: Ohio University Press, 1988.

Taylor, Michael J., ed. *The Mystery of Suffering and Death*. New York: Alba, 1973.

Teresa of Jesus. *The Life of Teresa of Jesus*. Trans. E. Allison Peers. Garden City, N.Y.: Image-Doubleday, 1960.

Thérèse of Lisieux. *The Autobiography of St. Therese of Lisieux*. Trans. John Beevers. Garden City, N.Y.: Image-Doubleday, 1957.

————. *Collected Letters of Saint Theresa of Lisieux*. Trans. F. J. Sheed.

Thielicke, Helmut. *Death and Life*. Trans. Edward Schroeder. Philadelphia: Fortress, 1976.

The Tibetan Book of the Dead. Trans. W. Y. Evans-Wentz. London: Oxford University Press, 1927.

Unamuno, Miguel de. *Tragic Sense of Life*. Trans. J. E. Crawford Flitch. New York: Dover, 1954.

Vanier, Jean. *The Broken Body*. New York: Paulist, 1988.

Van Zeller, Hubert. *Death in Other Words*. Springfield, Ill.: Templegate, 1983.

Von Balthasar, Hans Urs. *The Glory of the Lord: A Theological Aesthetics*. 7 vols. San Francisco: Ignatius Press, and New York: Crossroad, 1983–91.

———. *Life out of Death: Meditations on the Easter Liturgy*. Trans. Davis Perkins. Philadelphia: Fortress, 1985.

Von Hügel, Friedrich. *Eternal Life*. Edinburgh: T. and T. Clark 1912.

———. *The Mystical Element of Religion*. 2 vols. London: James Clarke, 1908.

Weil, Simone. *Waiting on God*. Trans. Emma Craufurd. London: Collins, 1959.

Wolff, Richard. *The Last Enemy*. Washington, D.C.: Canon, Press, 1974.

Zaehner, R. C. *Mysticism Sacred and Profane*. London: Oxford University Press, 1961.

INDEX

125